The WILL *to* HAPPINESS

The WILL to HAPPINESS

by Arnold A. Hutschnecker, M.D.

New Revised Edition

 Trident Press : *New York*

SBN: 671–27063–X

Library of Congress Catalog Card Number: 77–119497

Copyright, ©, 1964, 1970, by Arnold A. Hutschnecker

Published simultaneously in the United States and Canada by Trident Press, a division of Simon & Schuster, Inc., 630 Fifth Avenue, New York, N.Y. 10020

Printed in the United States of America

to T.E.

Contents

7

INTRODUCTION

A GREAT TRUTH SOMETIMES APPEARS SO SIMPLE THAT IT FAILS
to make an impression and therefore takes a long time to be
realized. The statement of one of my professors, a renowned
physiologist, that the "enjoyment of life is inborn in all
living beings," appeared to me such a simple truth that its
deeper meaning eluded me for over two decades. Overwhelmed by the responsibility of treating people in trouble,
but also thoroughly indoctrinated to consider pain, including the manifold aberrations of human failure, as a result of
some physical illness, I did not see the forest for the trees;
that is, I did not see the psychic background as a cause for
so many of my patients' afflictions.

Experience, perhaps, brought my professor's statement
back to my consciousness, and I began to wonder what has
happened to the alleged spontaneity of joy so often and so
remarkably absent in a doctor's office. Even if we assume
that the greater part of childish playfulness is channeled
into learning and work and all the other pursuits of adult
living, still, why are so comparatively few people able to
genuinely enjoy their existence? And what are the forces
that have the power to extinguish the capacity for joy which
appears to be natural in healthy children?

I related the same question to happiness, which is generally believed to depend on peak experiences of joy caused
either by fortunate outer events or inner gratifications.
While it is true, of course, that pleasurable experiences can
heighten our feelings of gladness or ecstasy, just as sad experiences can lower or seemingly extinguish these feelings,
happiness, I have come to believe, is a conscious awareness

9

of pleasure in people. It can be of different intensity as a result of different conditioned responses to set stimuli, differences that depend upon various or, we may say, conditioned degrees of inhibition. A preponderance of inhibition, then, can be called the cause for unhappiness.

"Happiness," as a word to describe a state of being, has become ambiguous through overuse. Some people regard happiness itself as an anachronism or fool's dream, inconsistent with the complexities and high pressure of our "civilized" way of life. "Sophisticated" people, therefore, seem to settle for terms such as "gratification" or "fulfillment." Others, incapable of love, often become cynical and equate a book that has "happiness" in its title with a sugar-coated panacea meant for gullible, simple-minded people.

Both the word and the state of being happy have become enigmatic to modern man—yet, there is no substitute for happiness. I believe there is no more intrinsic ambition in life than the achievement of personal happiness: this is the ultimate goal of every healthy human being.

While happiness may be an elusive topic about which to write, there comes a time when one cannot postpone a job just because it is difficult. Therefore, I have cognitively chosen for the theme of this book: happiness and the main causes of its devitalization.

In my very first book, *The Will to Live*, which was so generously endorsed by the medical profession and which found a large popular audience, I equated Freud's creative instinct with man's Will to Live, which is an innate chain of reflexes engaged in a continuous struggle against forces of self-destruction; the book's theme is survival. In this book, I shall examine the forces that determine man's Will to Happiness, which relates to the style and pleasures of life. Will is used here as an integrative power and as a decisive direction of energy toward a wholesome objective, not as a vague philosophical concept. It is not the same as willpower. From the standpoint of therapy, "will" will be used to indicate a successful change in a patient's behavior toward a productive and pleasurable existence.

In 1959, as a member of the United States Committee of the World Medical Association, I was privileged, with fifteen other American physicians, to go to the Soviet Union, where we had a chance to visit a number of hospitals and observe their different methods of treating physical, mental, and emotional problems. Three of us, including myself, were

10

admitted to the famous Pavlov Institute in Koltushi near Leningrad, heretofore generally closed to foreigners. Here I had an opportunity to learn about Pavlov's later work, which forms the basis for the study and treatment of chronically unhappy and mentally disturbed people in the East and which differs from the psychodynamic psychology practiced in the West.

Although I found some of the methods the Russian doctors used of immense interest and, from a treatment point of view, of great practical value, they do not reflect the depth of Freudian or other psychodynamic schools of thought. Freud's aim was to help the individual attain inner freedom and independence. These aims are, naturally, in conflict with any regime that exercises authoritarian control of the individual.

For instance, during an interview in Leningrad I asked the vice-director of the Bechterev Hospital, Professor Timofev, who is also chief psychiatrist of the Soviet Army, if Russian psychology accepted Freud's concept of the unconscious. He replied politely that Freudian psychoanalysis "is not allowed because we are not sure that he was right."

Only later did I learn that Pavlov, the Soviet Union's highly revered hero of science, had once said to a visiting American doctor, "Do you know that I was led to try these experiments by reading some of Freud's work?"—a statement obviously forgotten by the present generation of Russian doctors. Pavlov, on the other hand, was a classic experimenter who repeated his experiments over and over with scrupulous scientific exactness before he would allow himself to arrive at a conclusion.

Throughout this book I have attempted to integrate Pavlovian principles with our psychodynamic tenets. Although they are often regarded as contradictory to each other, they actually complement one another. In treating my patients I follow no dogma. I am guided by my years of experience and observation. My only considerations are: how can I make my patients become aware of their illness or their hidden self-destructive trends. And, having made them aware, how can I help them overcome the conditioning causing their unhappiness.

Inhibition as the greatest opponent and destroyer of happiness is not merely a vague term; it is a conditioned reflex, one that is acquired and can therefore also be discarded.

This then is the theme of this book: excitation is action,

11

and happiness is a purposeful release of energy toward a meaningful goal; inhibition is inaction, stagnation, and frustration, the various degrees of which determine our various states of unhappiness.

This concept will, I hope, explain why so many formulas which promise the achievement of happiness either fail or are superficial and can therefore have only a temporary effect. For it is understandable that if our automatic conditioning remains inwardly unchanged, all the moral virtues we practice and all the surface pleasures we seek to bring us happiness cannot really silence any inner unrest or conflict.

We shall explore the ways in which people come to know themselves so that they can detect and restore to a state of balanced functioning their over-excitation and over-inhibition. I shall leave unanswered a question Pavlov asked himself; namely, whether excitation and inhibition, the two so-intimately-interwoven functions of the nerve cells, are not fundamentally only different phases of one and the same physiochemical process. We need more knowledge before we can answer this question. But in the light of what we have learned so far, we can say that health and happiness are different expressions of one and the same concept. We shall concentrate therefore on the disturbing elements of this oneness and on the various causes of our unhappiness, for only by removing their causes can we expect to attain those pleasures which come from a free and purposeful release of energy. But this will require enough insight to recognize that the source of most of our trouble is in our inner conflicts rather than in disturbing outer conditions and obstacles.

Unhappiness is not merely a waste of one s own life, it is a threat to others, to our family and children, to our friends and associates. It is a burden to society, for unhappy people are dangerous people. They are restless, envious, resentful, distrustful, and filled with concealed hatred, even if they deny these feelings to themselves and to others. Unhappy people are dangerous people because they are carriers of the endemic disease called hostility.

The Hippocratic oath, I choose to believe, goes beyond a concern for the one single individual we as doctors happen to treat. Like illness, unhappiness in all its aspects is the doctor's concern. Consequently, I consider a book which aims to communicate experiences that may be of value to other people in trouble to be part of the doctor's job. This, however, brings him into conflict with his obligation to respect, under all and any circumstances, the confidences his patients have entrusted to him. And yet, what else can a doctor write about but his patients and his successful or unsuccessful treatments, if other people are to profit by them? This is how medicine has progressed. Other doctors who are authors and who have had the same problem have solved it, as have I, by retaining the essence of the problem but changing the outer details. Therefore, the cases in this book bear no resemblance to the patients who inspired them.

Sometimes a patient may say that he recognizes himself in the book and cannot believe that his particular problem is anything but unique. Then, too, one patient complained bitterly that he and his problem must have been too unimportant to be mentioned because he could not find himself in my first book. In spite of altered names and details, the involvements, the problems, the pain, and the anguish are genuine. Occasionally there may even be a situation of mistaken identity, but the dilemma of exercising integrity and at the same time presenting a case history as close to the reality as possible is one of the problems facing a doctor who is foolish enough to believe that he must compound his troubles by becoming an author. I shall not trouble the reader further with it except to repeat that I have attempted to write the truth, hoping that it will be useful to some troubled human being.

In my efforts to simplify the material and to organize it, I had the good fortune to have found the help of an editor who showed unfaltering enthusiasm, interest, and devotion throughout the years it took to prepare this book. Bud Christie deserves my respect and deepest gratitude for his patience, skill, and friendship.

I wish to thank the late Franz Alexander, the Nestor of psychosomatic medicine, for his permission to use, before its publication, his paper, "Experimental Study of Psychophysiological Correlations," which contains a study of seven psychosomatic diseases.

My thanks go to Dr. Ralph Jacoby and those of my colleagues who read the original manuscript and contributed invaluable points of criticism.

As much as books, conventions, and scientific papers help

to deepen a doctor's understanding, human experiences are really learned only in the quiet hours of rapport he has with his patients. Their touching honesty has earned my respect, and their so often senseless suffering has increased my determination to write this book.

A. A. H.

14

1.

PURSUIT of Happiness

> . . . *Only when we keep in mind the whole—the normal operation of one or another branch of an organism—can we differentiate without difficulty the accidental from the essential, the artificial from the natural; only then can we easily find new facts and often notice mistakes quickly.*
>
> —PAVLOV

WHEN, QUITE UNEXPECTEDLY, MY VERY FIRST PATIENT arrived as I was hanging the curtains in my New York home-office on East 82nd Street, I was faced with a propitious challenge to prove myself in this, the world's most competitive city. For here was a man who had been told, after a thorough hospital examination, that there was nothing organically wrong with him, yet still was complaining of stomach distress, insomnia, and a variety of other aches and pains. Not being pressured by time, I could listen, ask questions, examine him leisurely, and finally settle down to explain that his problems were due to his nerves. I called it "neurotic," because in 1936, when the incident took place, the term "psychosomatic" was not as yet much in use. I gave the man what I believed to be a good outline of the mind-body interrelationship, which I thought would explain to him the cause and effect of his troubles, remove his fears, and make him a happier human being.

I could not have been more surprised than to hear the man, who had listened with the utmost patience, ask me, "Doc, when do you want me to come back?"

Slightly puzzled, I remember replying, "My dear man, if you understood what I have tried to explain to you—never. You won't have to come back; you will be well." And my first patient left me pensively and for good.

I never learned if my forecast came true. But I have learned since then that it is rather naive to expect a purely

15

rational explanation to have any significant impact on a solidly established pattern of behavior. It may have worked with a well-adjusted man. Most likely such a person will not allow an emotional conflict to linger on until it produces physical symptoms. He will act or, if in a quandary, accept guidance and then act. The neurotically disturbed individual, however, would like to act but procrastinates for reasons of inner resistance, be it fear, guilt or shame or some other emotions unknown to him. Or he may escape the reality altogether by making himself blind to what the basic conflict is about and then use his illness as an excuse for his inability to act. One of the hardest facts for any young doctor to learn is to accept the fact that there are people who don't want to get well—and beyond this, that there are some people who actually want to die. It is tragic to listen to how some of the emotionally handicapped people—many of them physically strong—may exclaim as one young man did, "I was not taught how to fight nor how to live." And it is disturbing to watch the agony of people who are so paralyzed by fear that they cannot make themselves, as a Chinese proverb puts it, take that one first step with which a journey of a thousand miles begins.

A small boy of my acquaintance—and perhaps yours—pleads with his mother that he is too ill to go to school today and on this particular occasion she is persuaded. Then the message arrives: the examination scheduled for today has been postponed and an excursion to the seashore is to take its place. The boy is honestly indignant; he is mystified by his mother's unreasonableness when she does not allow him to join the excursion. He did feel sick before, and he does feel well now. His feelings are hurt that she does not believe him.

Man is said to be a reasoning animal—yet aroused emotions can only be felt or understood, never reasoned.

All of us must have known experiences similar to that of the little boy. Sometimes, even before we are wide awake in the morning, we are certain that we are coming down with something. Our throat may be sore, our head may ache, our eyes may burn or be blurred. We may have pains, especially in the back and legs. We may feel a heavy weariness even after a good night's sleep and are sure that we are running a fever. And sometimes, we may even know what it is we dread that makes us feel this way.

Some people may laugh it off and say, "It's probably psychosomatic," knowing very well that it definitely is psychosomatic. If the cause of our feeling disturbed is due to some unpleasant chore that must be done and we rouse ourselves to do it, it will soon be forgotten. But if. a chore violates our sense of pride or if, over a period of time, it has become a symbol of our rebellion against an authority or a parent or a boss or a domineering spouse, then the sum of these repressed angry responses can cause tensions and disturbances which are often accompanied by physical symptoms, like headaches, stomach pain, nausea, muscular spasm, palpitation of the heart, allergies etc.

Many remember the anger as a teenager when we were ordered to wash the dishes or to empty the garbage or to do some other chore just when we wanted to watch our favorite TV program and how we would grumpily drag our feet. We may take the attitudes of inner resistance into our adulthood and act out the negative feelings in a job, in a marriage or in a social situation, causing ourselves unhappiness. And we may learn at an early age what spurious tricks the human mind can play with bodily functioning. Yet, don't let us make the mistake of thinking that "psychosomatic" is the same as "imaginary" or "unreal." A psychosomatic illness, for all its absence of germs and seeming vagueness of origin, is real to the sufferer, a source of confusion, exhaustion and of infinite anxiety. It is a social problem as well as a problem of mental health.

A survey in midtown New York in 1962 revealed that only about 20 percent of the 160,000 people interviewed were considered adjusted, while the rest were termed more or less "neurotically disturbed." This condition, by no means restricted to the area where the census was taken, is a serious matter, for the sum of the mentally disturbed determines the mental health of a nation or the world at large.

The term "mental illness" still has a dreadful connotation. What is so frightening to many people is that the illness often seems to erupt suddenly and with full force. Sometimes it has a subtle beginning, then becomes more distinct and progressive. What at first appeared to be a minor maladjustment can and frequently does grow into a serious functional disability nourished by an exacerbation of a neurosis. Or we may have the outbreak of an acute mental illness.

We know that the best way to meet these problems is to recognize their existence and to achieve a healthy adjustment early. But sometimes we hear the question being asked how a sane adjustment can be attained if the home atmosphere had been a neurotic one—or, for that matter, is a sane adjustment at all possible in the insane world in which we live? To the environment of the madhouse only the madman can be said to be truly adjusted. What then is normal conduct?

While I was a premedical student I spent one semester away from my alma mater, the Friedrich Wilhelm University in Berlin, studying at the small, quaint university of Würzburg in Bavaria, a town with more baroque churches than any other its size, their clocks always running a little too fast or too slow and chiming every quarter hour. There I became acquainted with a fraternity life as antiquated as the buildings and their cobblestoned streets.

The "fox-major," a sort of drill sergeant and colonel in one, a referee in all matters pertaining to the rigid code of academic honor, made sharp and short speeches to his "foxes," the green newcomers.

Wearing white trousers tucked in soft, black boots reaching his thighs, a black velvet hussar jacket, and an embroidered cap which in other countries was worn by messenger boys, this arbiter of chivalry acquainted curious lads with what was honorable and proper academic behavior.

There, to drink ten tall glasses of beer in an evening was considered more "normal" than to drink but five glasses of this heavy, dark brew, and to show a strong bladder was more "manly" than to make frequent embarrassing visits to the bathroom. To be nonchalant about spending one's meager allowance was more "worldly" than to be anxious about money. And to meet at five o'clock in the morning in a deserted dance hall to watch or participate in a duel with a rapier or a sword, and to be casual about the sight and smell of fresh blood on an empty stomach was a sign of "courage." A scar on the cheek was prevented from healing properly by an extra heavy intake of beer, so that it would look big and grim, a symbol of "fearless" academic youth.

All this was "normal" behavior because it was traditional, even though one may not have liked it, as I did not. Translating the same sort of life to New York City, fighting a duel with swords would be considered ridiculous, barbaric and abnormal. Even in Würzburg, if a butcher or blacksmith had tried to duel it would have been considered presumptuous, comical, and "abnormal." The police would not have hesitated to make arrests.

Dueling with swords is not considered normal conduct in most of the civilized world, certainly not in the last part of the twentieth century, but what *is* normal is *an adjustment to the environment, whatever it might be.* The people in England and other countries even adjusted to life under bombardment during World War II, and in most countries the adjustment was so surprisingly good that the statistics for mental illness actually took a turn downward. It is almost as if mankind can live better in adversity than in peace, comfort, and prosperity.

Where there is maladjustment and psychosomatic illness, we must attempt to understand what in a person's emotional makeup is healthy and what is neurotic and why it is often so difficult for one human to adjust to another human being. We are so ready to blame the difficulty on the obstinacy of the other and not to see the rigidity in ourselves. Why are we often so blind and why are we so defensive? Because we react, as we shall see, according to our first conditioning which takes place when we know of no moral or other inhibiting values and are motivated by one great need: "Give me—me, me, me."

A woman came to me in distress. She had recently suffered several fainting spells, and she had been overwrought and depressed over a period of weeks because of a sharp disagreement with her husband which both were unable to resolve. An attractive widow in her early forties, she had married a widower fifteen years her senior.

Both claimed to have been very happy in their first marriages, and this one was approved by their rather large circle of mutual friends. My patient was very anxious to make this relationship work. But in spite of her efforts and good intentions, trouble developed not long after their honeymoon. The specific cause of it was an elderly friend of hers, a woman in her seventies, who had been a lifelong friend of my patient's mother and to whom her new husband had taken violent objection. Recently this elderly friend, who had come for dinner, stayed overnight because of a snowstorm, whereupon the husband moved out to his

19

club. The tensions had become unbearable, and, unhappily, the wife began to think in terms of separation.

I saw the husband only once. He came to me mainly because of concern over his wife's health. He acted as if he knew of no problem between them and dismissed rather tersely my question whether he was jealous or had any objection to his wife's friendship with the older woman. I did not feel that he was giving me his full confidence about the problem, but I was satisfied about his genuine concern for his wife's welfare.

His wife, on the other hand, was not conscious of the fact that she too was not being quite open. She should have known that when she married this man she could not expect of him the elasticity of youth in the necessary period of adjustment. Concerned about her own needs, she failed to understand the insecurity in her husband, so that instead of helping him to overcome his problems, she increased them. Just as she could not expect to change the world, or her husband, she had to change toward him.

There was no need for her to break with her maternal friend and then, in silence, to resent it. There was no need to make this relationship a test case, even if her anxiety demanded a mother substitute, and to pursue a policy of "If I don't assert myself from the very start, I will be fully swallowed up." And there was no need for her to provoke her husband by her defiance in seeing her elderly friend. "*Si vis amari ama,*" said Seneca, the Roman Stoic—"If you wish to be loved, love." If both people had from the very beginning practiced this formula, obstacles could not have developed. It was in herself, not in her husband, that this woman had to find the success of her second marriage as, I have no doubt, she had in her first.

She came to my office on her first visit, as quite a few people do, in search of a pill to soothe her nerves, possibly wanting me to act as an older brother who would tell off her recalcitrant husband. She suffered from a variety of distressing symptoms, as do most people who repress their anger and whose inhibitions devour immense stores of energy, which otherwise would be available for happier living. Dimly aware of the existing inner conflicts she was craving for drugs to replace the missing energy. She, like many other people, hoped to restore a state of balanced functioning quickly and effortlessly by just a pill.

My patient had to be made aware that, like a little girl, she wanted to have her cake and eat it too. She wanted to be married because of her feelings of loneliness and she wanted to be married to this particular man because of his social prominence and wealth. It gave her pleasure to prove to him and others how well she could run his home. Beyond this she gave nothing of herself. Her husband's emotional immaturity did not help matters. His pride and external behavior of independence did not allow him to ask for the affection he craved. Feeling deprived, he turned his anger against his wife's friend to relieve the rising sense of failure in his new marriage. Both dreaded a divorce. Both were eager to continue to display to their friends a good show of happiness rather than to come to grips with their fundamental problems. And so, they reached a compromise which made them neither terribly happy nor terribly unhappy. They were ahead of millions of other people who do not even come near to reaching a compromise, and therefore remain in a state of conflict which makes them feel tense, tired and exhausted most of the time. They turn to drugs.

To meet their daily obligations many of these discontented people keep themselves "up" with a stimulant, then relax their overstrained nerves with a counter drug to give them tranquility. This indicates that they have either lost or impaired that inner regulating power which aims to balance bodily functioning as automatically as, for instance, the central nervous system, which regulates the body temperature, water metabolism, stimulation and inhibition of the hormone glandular system, and so on. The great advance of chemistry has produced a legion of new and at times very effective drugs, which have taken the place of the older sedatives and sleeping pills. Anxiety—diffuse, inner fear—is a state of arousal to meet an emergency which either does not exist in reality or which is grossly exaggerated. The counteraction is a balancing process of inhibition, which is automatic in the normal individual but disturbed or lost in the neurotically disturbed personality. And so, tranquilizers have been developed. They can, indeed, calm the individual to a point where he can view his situation more objectively. But they also can make an individual so overconfident that he may lose the censorship of good judgment.

While it would be displaying childish bravado for a man in a state of acute stress to refuse to take advantage of these

medicines, it would on the other hand be dangerously ne-
glectful to fail to recognize the deeper meaning of the signal
of stress, and, by eating tranquilizers, support a means of
escape rather than attempt to understand the existence of a
disturbing conflict and try to resolve it.

Mental states more serious than anxiety are the various
types of depression. Depressed people have a difficulty to
function. They show a loss of interest, a loss of initiative as
well as an inability to experience joy. They either fear death
or unconsiously desire death as a relief from suffering. For
about one and a half decades now, a new type of drug has
come into existence—the energizers or anti-depressant drugs.
These drugs play quite a different and a rather specific role
in relieving symptoms of mental depression or even curing
depressed mental states. They repair, chemically, a disturbed metabolic function, but, as with tranquilizers, they
do not really cure a basically negative outlook on life.
Therefore, once a person is out of his state of depression, a
happier relationship with his environment must be established, either by the efforts of the individual himself or with
the help of a doctor.

The history of anti-depressant drugs has in one decade
revolutionized medicine. Heretofore hopeless people are
being restored to normal or near normal functioning. It has
also given us evidence of how often depressed states sail
under the flags of physical illness or discomforts such as
sleep disturbances, early awakening, rumination, constipa-
tion, loss of weight and appetite, fatigue, urinary frequency,
decreased libido, palpitations, headaches, menstrual changes,
and so on. Or, they often express themselves by emotional symptoms such as feeling "low" or "blue" or sad,
guilty, unworthy, hopeless, or anxious, or by an overread-
iness to cry, by experiencing some inner terror, a fear of
death or of disease, or undue worry over the past or the
future. Other symptoms are poor concentration, indeci-
siveness, a loss of memory, states of confusion and significantly a loss of sexual interest.

Except for the mentally ill and, more specifically, the
acute psychotics, as well as for those people in melancholic
states due to the loss of a mate, or a close friend, the onset
of a depression may often not be recognized. A depression is
a frightening experience, like a slowly growing state of paralysis. It is a time to seek help in order to understand what

repressed rage or indecision or terror is tearing us apart. This is necessary so that we can move to resolve the inner conflict and thereby help mind and body to restore a state of balanced functioning. Today, practically every physician is familiar with the symptoms and knows about the cure.

A few years after the end of World War II a young man came to me in a very anxious and depressed state. It was before we had the new anti-depressant drugs. The choice of treatments then was to give stimulants like the amphetamines or the "happy pills" or, in severe cases, electric shock. Speaking about his very unhappy life, it seemed that the patient's mother was at the root of his anguish. At that time he was a war veteran, a law-school graduate, a man who had a brilliant intellect and should have been making and taking his own way in the world. But his mother was still treating him as she had when he was a boy, passive and compliant.

As far back as he could remember, his mother had been the tyrant of their household. As a rule her authority was unquestioned; whenever it was challenged to any extent, she became sick, with doctors and nurses in attendance while the rest of the household tiptoed and whispered to avoid disturbing the patient. Thus she dictated to father and son, never defeated, and, as they became accustomed to her rule and repeated victories, they learned to avoid the battle if it was at all possible. Twice the youth considered marriage and twice he withdrew in the face of maternal objections.

Now an even more serious crisis loomed in his life. His father was also a lawyer, and the mother wanted the son to go to work in his father's firm. The young man felt that to do so would be to surrender forever his right to assert himself. Since the father was completely dominated by the mother, he felt that it was most important for him to find a place in some other law firm, where he would be independent of his father as well as his mother and could develop into a respected and successful lawyer. His mother said that if he did become associated with any firm except his father's it would be a disgrace and would most likely kill her. No crisis had occurred yet because, though he had been trying for almost a year, he had not been able to land a job.

He did not know at first why he had failed to find a position in view of his superior law school and army record.

"It must be me," he said finally in despair. "I must blow my chances." And, indeed, he admitted that during interviews he felt himself freezing up and becoming tongue-tied, the same way he had felt when years ago his mother asked him to give an accounting of what he had done. But even before going into an interview, he said, "I experience an unbearable anxiety. I have caught myself thinking of what would happen to her if I should get the job. Would she die? Would I not have killed her? Then I behave like a stammering idiot. I know that I am probably much better qualified than the fellow who gets the job, but I can't help it. I see what goes on and I am powerless to move."

He had an appointment for another interview on the following morning and he said, "If I don't make it this time, I'm through. I have been to all the good firms, and I might just as well give in and accept my lot." He was not too hopeful that a combination tranquilizer and pep pill would do him much good or stop his terrifying panic, but he was desperate, ready to grasp at any straw. We had to rehearse how he would straighten up and walk into the room and sit down.

Some of the drugs developed since the Second World War are most effective for various psychosomatic conditions but, like crutches and splints, they must be considered emergency measures and not cures. I am glad to prescribe them for emergencies and during the period of readjustment. The young man knew that he would have to hold down his job after obtaining it, and that he could not depend on pills. But right now he had to overcome his first serious obstacle and he did. He got the job. But he wanted to know more about himself, and his fears and inhibitions. He knew that he had to free himself from his clutching mother, but he did not know how.

The young lawyer is an excellent example of the proverbial cliché of the Silver Cord theme well known in life and extensively described in literature. A mother is often demanding and selfish enough to make all other members of her family fearful and miserably unhappy. Although it is a sad fact that mothers often have a destructive influence on their children and distort their values, and although a mother's demands may be unreasonable, her position as a mother gives her an almost unlimited power to mold the young mind according to her own image. The seeds she plants by

24

her teachings and more so by the examples she gives by her own behavior, including her fears, guilts, and distorted point of view—all these things take firm hold in a child's mind, where they ripen into full destructive bloom. The struggle of the growing human to free himself is often hard and bitter. Fear and guilt are powerful means of control; they are not easily shaken. But man has a free will, and at some time in his life he will have to free himself from her domination. He must accept his responsibility and stop blaming his mother. In all likelihood, she may have been enslaved by her own mother, an observation which obviously prompted Victor Hugo to say, "If you want to reform a man you must begin with his grandmother."

In the case of our young lawyer, we found that it was not just his fear of what would happen to his mother or her objections that stood between him and the new life symbolized by the job he wanted. It was not really his mother who stood between him and his desire. He stood in his own way, not because of his fear of what might happen to his mother, but because of his fear of what might happen to *him* if something happened to her. So dependent was he that, while he desired freedom, he also feared that selfsame independence. So long as he saw the problem in terms of his mother as the obstacle to his desire, the young man was helpless. But when he understood that it was he himself who made the problem, he was then able to recognize the true choice that lay before him, and, knowing that, the decision he had to make was clear.

Did he want to take the risk of possibly hurting his mother, then suffer guilt for the rest of his life? Or did he prefer to avoid that risk and instead accept a lifelong state of dependency, even after his mother's eventual death, should he survive that? The struggle for independence is not only natural, it is the only chance the individual has to pursue a life of health and happiness. A parent's protectiveness must come to an end at the time the growing child has attained the independence necessary to secure his own survival so that he can fight his own battles.

Our young lawyer found that putting into effect what he had learned intellectually, turned out to be a long, arduous and painful endeavor. He sometimes wavered in his many struggles with his conscience. But he was determined. He married the girl of his choice against the opposition of his parents, who refused to come to his wedding, and he discontinued seeing me as soon as he felt he could manage by himself. The great lesson he learned was that true parental love means letting go of one's child; neurotic love is holding on to the child. The other lesson he learned was that regardless of how much a woman may strive to dominate, basically she wants the man to stop her aggression and domination and she will love the man who can do it, even if the man happens to be her own son.

2.

The GORDIAN Knot

A MARRIED WOMAN, TODAY THIRTY-FOUR YEARS OLD AND the mother of two children, came to New York some years ago single, attractive, the world before her, and with hopes of a theatrical career in her heart. Now, instead, she sits in a doctor's office, cataloguing her complaints:

"Fatigue, a kind of heavy, leaden feeling, holds my body down. It seems never to leave me lately, and it is a struggle to get out of bed. At times migraine headaches come unannounced and nothing can be done about them. Even when there is no headache my head feels tight, as if held by an iron band."

Overweight, she wondered if anything could really be done about it. Many diets, she regretted to say, never really worked for her. Was there such a thing as a happy marriage? Were there any real men left today? She had two children, she said, then corrected herself: three, referring to her husband as differing only in size from the other children.

Her work she had come to resent, not only because it had become such a bore, but because by now she wanted to be a woman, to be taken care of. But her husband, a commercial artist, was in and out of work, free-lancing. Now that she has proven herself stronger than he, what good did it do her?

Did she ever allow herself to be angry? She never really dared to express her hostility. She did not believe in pounding tables or yelling or throwing tantrums; her husband could do all this much more expertly. It was evident that this woman hated in silence, that she was a martyr about many things, and that she considered hate to be sinful. Sinful, uncivilized and unladylike. Her description of the many physicians who had treated her—unsuccessfully, as she pointed out—was a subtle expression of her hostility. She did not dare to reveal such a feeling openly, but she could tell a doctor that his pills did not do her any good.

We see a woman who, living for many years with ambitions, now finds herself in middle life without having come near their fulfillment, feeling increasingly disappointed and confused, and considering herself as a failure.

Another patient, a woman who strayed close to the borderline of cracking up, was the mother of four children, who had been treated for toxic goiter and gastro-intestinal complaints. Above all, she was deeply troubled by chronic anxiety and unhappiness from her childhood on. She blamed her troubles mainly on her impatient, rigid, and domineering husband, and felt trapped by her unhappy marriage. To dissolve the marriage was out of the question because she was in need of the protection her husband provided for her. She was afraid of being alone and of the responsibility she would have to assume. Also, the thought of causing her children unhappiness was frightening and unacceptable. Yet, continuing the marriage, which she felt lacked any real and warm communication, meant to continue an unhappy existence, and her unrelieved nervous tension was causing her bodily suffering. She saw no way out, and she felt depressed when some doctors and her own husband called her a hypochondriac.

The woman had married upon the urging of an older sister, who acted as a mother substitute, and when the patient dared to express a mild protest, the sister derided her and only further undermined her already shaky self-confidence. Therefore, in order to cease being a burden to the home, she was ready for any escape. She married for security more than for love. Her husband provided the security. She really had no justifiable complaint about him, except that he was a jealous man who yelled a great deal. But the lack of any real fault on his part only intensified rather than diminished her unhappiness. Now it seemed that she was trapped in life by a decision made in the past, a sadly wrong, yet irrevocable decision.

It was true enough that nothing now could change that decision. Even divorce would not alter the fact that the marriage had produced four children. Nor was she sure, deep down, whether she had not reason to blame herself.

Some women, she tried to console herself are perhaps born more frigid than others and must therefore endure unrestrained male selfishness. She rationalized that she just was an unhappy person by nature and also that by nature she was born with no interest in sex and as she grew up had come to detest it. In her case, it was unlikely that divorce would help because of her intense dependency needs. Instead of correcting her unhappy situation, it could intensify it by unconsciously increasing her feelings of failure and guilt. Indeed, if nothing within the emotional and mental makeup of a person who is structured like our patient changes, he or she repeats, as we so often see, their unhappy pattern in a new marriage.

Still another patient, a fifty-five-year-old businessman came to my office, because of his depression. He claimed that he had lost his inner drive. He had become easily irritated, impatient and was terrified to find that he was losing his self-control. Life had become wearing. What should be meaningful—work, family, friends—no longer gave him pleasure.

This is the reason he gave for what he thought had caused his unhappy state of mind: his brother, who was two years his senior, had died about eighteen months earlier. Their relationship had been an unusually intimate and harmonious one and therefore his brother's death had shaken him profoundly. The two men had been in business together, and in all the many years they had never had any real points of disagreement.

Now, his dead brother's wife made demands affecting the running of the business. My patient could not agree with the wisdom of these suggestions, and he therefore finally decided to hand over his stock to his sister-in-law, for he felt that unless he could run the company in his way its existence would be in jeopardy. At this point his sister-in-law was afraid to take over and admitted that she could not handle the responsibilities involved. She knew that her brother-in-law was a most capable and wise businessman, and yet she continued to oppose him with ideas of her own.

Her persistent interference had created a deep and distressing conflict in my patient, who felt he owed it to his brother to respect his widow's wishes, although he knew that disaster would overtake all if he were to listen to her suggestions. His grief, his conscience, and perhaps some unconscious guilt feelings, whether justified in reality or not, created a problem so intense that it began to wear him down.

Throughout his life, the patient said, he had been able to evaluate a situation and, after some deliberation, had been able to act. The present problem was a novel and bewildering experience. He could not remember ever having been caught in a trap like the one he was in now or having felt as frustrated by indecision as at the present time. He could not rebuke his sister-in-law, and he could not submit to her wishes—nor could he allow himself to be angry.

These three cases—a woman trapped by life, another woman regretting a past that she is now unable to change, and a man unable to make a decision about something important enough to affect his happiness—are not unusual or extreme examples but fairly representative of the psychosomatic causes of illness that frequently come to doctors' attention. These persons go over and over the same questions in their minds without being able to reach a conclusion.

There is no intention here to say that these problems do not exist or are not important or can be wished away. Let us admit that there is no way to reach a simple conclusion for any of these people. These are problems for which there is seemingly no "solution." The morning news is often full of such dilemmas. Yet somehow the individual must solve the conflict and establish some working relationship with the people he is involved with if he is to survive.

Man produces energy. This energy he must release in order to stay well. If the released energy satisfies his needs or ambitions and leads to a meaningful goal, he will feel happy. If he does not know where to pour out his energy because he has no goal or direction or because he cannot make a decision, the force of this energy is turned against himself, leading to tension, illness, and unhappiness. The myth of the Gordian Knot well illustrates the point I wish to make—for the knot which could not be untied symbolized a problem that cannot be solved.

Gordius, being made king, dedicated his wagon to the deity of the oracle and tied it up in its place with a fast knot. This was the celebrated Gordian Knot of which it was said in later times that whoever should untie it would become lord of all Asia. Many tried to untie it, but none succeeded until Alexander the Macedonian, later surnamed the Great, came to Phrygia eager to embark on a career of conquest. He tried his skill with as little success as the others, until, growing impatient, he drew his sword and cut the knot. When he afterwards succeeded in subjecting all Asia to his sway, people began to think that he had complied with the terms of the oracle according to its true meaning.

Perhaps what the oracle had intended, since the knot could not be untied, was that no one ever should be lord of all Asia, or it may have meant what Alexander had demonstrated, that sometimes a clean cut is the only sensible solution to a difficult problem. If we apply the symbol of the Gordian Knot to any of the complicated situations life is so full of, we must resolve that man cannot allow himself to be guided by an oracle or limit his course by the seeming complexity of a problem. Inhibition is a step towards death. We must, therefore, in order to live, find a way which allows us a release of our energies. Alexander gave us a classic example by making a decision and by not hesitating to act.

The Gordian Knot of the first patient, the woman who had a weak and passive-dependent husband, consisted in her confused sense of loyalty and concern for her children, which blocked her action. Once she realized that he would not change and that she was sacrificing her health and happiness as well as that of her children for an unrealistic dream, she could gather her strength to cut herself free.

The second patient, the woman who was too frightened and passive to consider seriously a separation, had to learn to give more of herself if she wanted to be a healthier and happier person. Like the woman in the previous chapter she wanted her cake and to eat it too. To cut her Gordian Knot meant to cut herself free from the image of her own immature self-pitying, martyr-like mother and grow into a more mature, giving, loving woman.

The last patient had to cut through his neurotic hesitation and paralysis of action by having transferred the love for his brother to his sister-in-law. He had to resist the immature and grandiose ideas of his sister-in-law and continue to run the company with the experience and efficiency he had shown in the past.

The symbol of the Gordian Knot then teaches us, that cutting a Gordian Knot does not necessarily mean severing

31

ties we have formed through close relationships, but, rather, severing those ties of bondage we have developed during our formative years which are preventing our growth and which we so often transfer to other people, a wife, a husband, or a friend. Unless we cut ourselves free we are bound to continue in a pattern of enslavement. This may eventually lead to rebellious uprisings and breaking of relationships by divorce or detachment. Only the truly free and independent individual can allow himself to enter into a close relationship with another human being, including a mature friendship with his parents. This is the aim which sometimes demands an operational sunderance, as symbolized by the cutting of the Gordian Knot.

3.

NERVOUS BREAKDOWN

ALEXANDER THE GREAT IS SAID TO HAVE WEPT WHEN there were no more worlds for him to conquer. Even he, who gave the appearance of being a man of strength broke down when there were no more decisions to be made and no actions to be taken. He sought diversion in pleasure and eventually revisited Babylon to prove his supremacy. There, with evidently no real will to live left in him, he died at the height of his glory from an infection at the age of thirty-two. He had not matured to discharge his energies toward new, creative human goals.

But the Gordian Knot that is associated with his name lives on as a symbol for apparently insoluble problems. It teaches us that when an intricate or "knotty" problem remains unresolved, when a person fails to cut through the maze of an existing deep seated conflict and thereby continues to be bombarded by pressures from within or from without, nature takes a hand and causes a physical or mental breakdown. Such a disruption of any organized functioning—which signifies a breakdown—occurs in order to prevent the unbearable tensions to damage the body beyond repair. A breakdown is in essence a curative tendency in a human who does not want to die. Most people come out of a breakdown with greater clarity or a new philosophy of life.

There are other people who, unknown to themselves, resist the innate healing power of nature and remain sick. Many of these people really don't want to die, but they cannot live with any sense of enjoyment either. When being told about their self-destructive way of life, the greater number of these people tend to reject the idea that what they call their old nervous habits—like driving themselves, or overeating, smoking or drinking too much—are actually tiny little steps toward death. Just because their robust physical constitution may take the punishment to their body for many years without visible harm, they delude themselves that it may perhaps destroy another fellow but that they themselves might get away with it. It seems that more people than not simply lack the ability to create their own happiness and lack therefore a reverence for their own life. Some people, after some brush with death or after having had a breakdown, will give their life meaning and recover by their own efforts; others may eventually lose their grip on life and linger on, being neither well nor overtly sick.

To the physiologist, life is cell damage and repair. To sustain life, all cells must fulfill specific functions whereby they expend energy. Expenditure of energy damages cells; nourishment repairs them. Most of the body's cells are constantly being destroyed and at the same rate replaced. Blood and skin cells are of this order. But others are not replaceable; brain cells are among these. For this reason the destruction of brain cells has serious though not always fatal consequences. The body ceaselessly applies protective mechanisms to prevent a destruction of the brain cells in order to maintain life. When cell damage, through relentless stress, exceeds repair to the point of being irreparable, then normal brain function becomes impaired or it stops altogether. It is in this way that the healthy organism forces an individual to have the rest necessary for repair to overtake the damage. The creature falls asleep, or continues to move in a daze or plunges into unconsciousness.

Thus, a conflict that remains unresolved may lead to states of exhaustion and prepare the ground for a breakdown. Some patients, when they give their history prior to their breakdown, deny or minimize the existence of a conflict. Often they admit that they worried too much or worked too hard for too long a time without rest. Others may say that they had tried to cope with some distressing conditions of a job or a personal involvement, or problems of sex such as dissatisfaction or frustration until they could not take it any longer and then just went to pieces. A patient of mine who had lost her only son in an accident said, a year later, "that she must have had a breakdown because she had been walking around all the time in a kind of a numb state, spending days in bed, not caring to eat, neglecting herself, forgetting things, and enjoying nothing."

There is one never failing advance symptom of a breakdown: *Unhappiness.* When people cannot enjoy themselves, when genuine laughter has become an experience of the past and their daily lives become more of a burden to them than an existence filled with little pleasure and conquests, then they are depressed. Happiness cannot exist when we lose our will to live or when we are chronically angry or fearful. Or when we live with anxiety and frustration. Therefore, the onset of a breakdown can be recognized when an individual begins to show a persistent change away from his inherited or conditioned temperamental type of joyful behavior; or when such a person begins to exhibit a loss of control of his physical or his mental functioning or both. We may then observe shortness of temper, quick hostile responses, or listlessness, lack of interest or concentration, absent-mindedness, compulsive weeping, affective mood swings, depressive states, and, in more serious cases, thought disorders.

There may be physical symptoms of feeling tired all the time, of not being able to sleep, of restlessness or of neurotic conversions, as in conversion hysteria, without organic changes. Or we may find a loss of sexual interest, of impotence or frigidity, or of a variety of psychosomatic illnesses with or without organic changes. In the case of organic changes we may have a coronary attack, a cerebral hemorrhage, a peptic ulcer, an arthritic episode, colitis, a bleeding ulcer or some other illnesses. These symptoms may be precipitated or aggravated by emotional stress. If there is an absence of physical symptoms, if we find an individual ceasing to be productive, and having symptoms of dullness and apathy in place of his creative ability, then his healthy pursuit of happiness is on the decline while the creative drive is being side-tracked or destroyed by an unresolved conflict.

The healthy person can recognize the danger and deal with it by fight or flight—the neurotically inhibited person remains in a state of fright or fearful indecision. In such a state the individual can get ahold of himself by his own efforts or by seeking help, and thereby bring about a change

35

in the tangle of his life. He must cut his Gordian Knot, which means, he must end a destructive relationship or situation if he wishes to avoid a mental breakdown. Channelling his creative energies out by doing something that has meaning, putting interest in one's job, assuming a positive attitude towards the responsibilities of an adult life, concerning oneself with the affairs of one's community or one's country, or participating in a town meeting or serving on some committee. All or any of these activities are helpful, but a real and more permanent sense of happiness can come only from an intimate involvement with another human being, as in a man-woman, husband-wife, parent-child relationship. Or we may derive happiness in a mature friendship by sharing of interests, or work or play. In a simple way we can release energy and thereby enjoy ourselves by doing something around the house, like doing repairs, or painting, or cooking, or gardening, or hooking a rug, or answering a letter. Anything that allows physical or psychic energy to be channelled out constructively is healthy and can prevent such energy from being turned destructively against the self. If, on the other hand, the person remains indecisive and thereby does not stop the downhill trend, he must in due time lose control of his life.

There are many causes which, when unrelieved, can break down and destroy a body, such as man's ancient curses of hunger and disease. Or exposure to heat or cold. Or war. Or accidents. But the breakdown we are talking about here is a break of a person's will or his break with reality—even if these breaks are short-lived. Many of the reasons which cause a breakdown are manufactured by the individual himself. There are, however, deeper causes over which an individual has little control and which are part of his psychic makeup or his emotional constitution with or without organic or chemical pathology. The disturbances can range from neurotic states like emotional immaturities to the more serious pathological, psychotic episodes where there is a break with reality and a disintegration of the personality. The more serious cases require psychiatric help or treatment in mental institutions.

The less serious disturbances, with which we shall concern ourselves, are states of unhappiness and those conditions which bring about a cessation of a person's organized functioning, the little breakdowns in life, whether temporary or over a longer period of time. These are periods during which a person may feel that he can no longer cope with the demands made on him. Among them we have the various forms of sexual maladjustment. Or the intense socio-economic struggle. We have the problem of boredom, of aging and the fear of death.

There is a proneness to breakdowns in people who cannot love and who cannot relate affectionately to another human being, in both the heterosexual but more so in the homosexual life. Or among the many troubled people who are pressured by some or by many hidden fears and distrusts and by those who suffer anxiety desiring but fearing human closeness.

Still another area leading to breakdowns are the addictions like the over-use of alcohol, of narcotics, or a variety of drugs people use to get through the day or the fears of night. Many physicians, including this author, believe however, that the overuse of drugs or alcohol is more a result of some deep, inner stress than its cause.

A nervous breakdown may appear in various forms, and the various forms may have different degrees. Besides the obsessive-compulsive symptoms we have mentioned—like overwork, overeating—there may be gambling or a compulsive spending of money beyond one's means and other neurotic symptoms. When an individual feels relentlessly driven from within, he seeks release from such pressures. One man may have been able to repress his immense tensions or rage until his controls break one day and then there may be violence, or he may begin to drink without stop and end up on skid row. One patient never kept his appointment. Unable to cut his neurotic relationship with a seemingly loving yet strong and domineering mother, after a visit with her he drove against a tree and was killed instantly. Another person may have a less serious accident, or he may, for other reasons, land in a hospital. He may even know that the accident was no accident, or he may deny this fact. I have known a young mother suddenly to go on a wild spending spree to the point where she misused money meant for her children's food and bought things she did not need. As a child she had grown up barefoot, and her flight from reality took the form of a compulsion to spend all her money on expensive shoes, ending up with some hundred pairs of them and a huge pile of debts.

Another form of release from tension may lead to symptoms of conversion. The repressed impulses of a conflict are converted into somatic symptoms, such as the psychogenic paralysis of a limb, which prevents the aggressive acting out of a socially undesirable fantasy.

And then we have the vast number of psychosomatic illnesses, with or without organic changes. This "legitimate" kind of breakdown respects the conventional concept, which considers a physical illness beyond anyone's control whereas a nervous or mental breakdown is frowned upon and often equated with weakness of character. By means of psychosomatic illness, a person may be able to obtain a cessation from an inner emotional battle and win time for repairwork, while at the same time gaining the sympathy he wants and above all preserve his self-respect.

It is not an attempt to be facetious when I say that in many instances a patient actually needs a nervous breakdown in order to avoid more serious or irreparable damage to himself. The breakdown may be a short or prolonged "breathing spell" which allows the person to get out of the crossfire of his conflicts or some other intolerable life situation.

Such a patient came to see me. He was a sophisticated, forty-year old businessman who, a few months prior to his first visit to my office, had suffered a heart attack which his doctor at first thought was a coronary occlusion but later interpreted as a sort of breakdown without organic consequences. This incident had shaken up the patient quite badly. He now lived with a constant fear which he tried desperately to conceal but which he made evident by frequent, furtive attempts to count his pulse, carefully hiding his wrist below the table level.

This patient was an angry man. There were many angers, but right now he was angry with himself because his strength and will power had left him. He was afraid that he might at any moment reveal in public his hostility or his readiness to weep. Before this point in his life he thought he had known pretty well what he wanted, but now he did not know anything or what he was doing or where he was going. His trouble had first come to his conscious awareness as a terrible pain in his chest one night just after he had gone to bed. He felt that he could not breathe, and he broke out in a cold sweat.

At first he thought he had indigestion, but the pain persisted, and his wife called a doctor, who ordered him into a hospital the same night. There he was kept for three weeks. Eventually he was told that no evidence of an organic illness could be found. This news should have delighted him, but actually it made him feel upset, confused and ashamed. He admitted to me how much he had feared his wife's derision.

The attack had come on very suddenly and for no obvious reasons. Later he remembered an incident with a client which had greatly upset him. He now wondered if the excitement could have caused his heart attack. This is how the patient described the incident:

He was the head of his own and only moderately successful record producing firm. A few days prior to the attack he had a heated telephone conversation with a client who blamed him for a considerable loss of money. This denunciation, the patient felt, was a most unfair distortion of the facts, yet, since the client was more powerful than he, he did not really dare to argue his point. He felt his reputation in the business world was at stake. Angered and frustrated, he began to brood about the injustice and the disgrace, blaming himself that perhaps he should not have conceded to his client quite as much as he did.

The unfortunate business experience grew into a huge problem, adding another obstacle to his enfeebled pursuit of happiness that was already impeded by his inner insecurity and by outer problems such as his financial worries and the unhappy relationship with his wife. "You sure took the hard way to prove your point," was her comment the day after the attack when she came to the hospital to see him.

When he left the hospital, he was depressed. The doctor who treated him had impressed upon him the need to take it easy, to slow down. He had given him a long list of prohibitions, all of which disturbed him greatly because it made him feel like an invalid. He thought that the creative period of his life had ended.

In time he saw another doctor who suggested a more permissive program, pointing out the actual dangers of a too restricted one. This doctor interpreted the attack as a psychosomatic kind of nervous breakdown. The patient was told that he could do physically anything he wanted to but should stop as soon as any disturbing symptom appeared.

This made him feel better but it could neither relieve nor explain his anxieties.

Recalling his childhood years, he remembered that his mother had been very much upset when he was about five because he was discovered to have a functional heart murmur. She repeatedly impressed upon him the need to be "careful". This sounded like the advice the doctor had given him while he was in the hospital, or, rather, the doctor sounded like his mother. He was not conscious that the early warnings to be careful about his heart had stayed with him, nor of the importance he had attached to the fact that his father had died of a coronary occlusion.

This patient had no heart ailment. The psychosomatic illness was a face-saving device, though shortlived and inadequate. He had suffered a breakdown.

What is the nature of a breakdown? How does it come about? Our bodily responses are closely associated with the mental and emotional functioning of our personalities. All the organs, all the parts of the body—as Pavlov, Nobel Prize winner and world-renowned physiologist, demonstrated—have tiny centers of representation in the multi-billion outer layers of the brain. This explains physiologically what the psychologists have known from experience, that each injury to the body has a corresponding trauma in the brain.

It is significant that injury to the mind and the scars of the traumatic experiences we have lived through during our formative years are not like the injuries to the body. They remain hidden, "forgotten" and guarded against. Scars of the mind, while covered up with layers of compensating behavior, affect our responses and cause specific reactions, the sum of which in due time make up our personality. These processes do not only relate to the way we butter our bread, but to all the complex ways in which we have learned to deal with other people, be it an initial warm receptiveness, a friendly grin, a quick withdrawal, a sharp cynical joke, or an aloof behavior.

Claude Bernard, the great French biologist, came to the conclusion that illness was the result of a faulty adaption to noxious agents. The adaptive defense reaction originally was meant to help the organism in its battle against destructive elements, but if this adaptive defense reaction continued to exist beyond its original need it became a damaging force in itself. For instance, every organism responds to danger with an extra output of adrenalin, which in turn produces a rise of the blood pressure. However, if we deal with an over-adaptation to a threat, real or imaginary, we may overstimulate the nervous and glandular systems, and retain the elevated pressure over a prolonged period of time, although the threat, in reality, may have long ceased to exist.

In a similar way, a symptom of adaptation with regard to our emotional reactions may turn into a disease of adaptation. If, for instance, a child finds that he can easily get out of a tight spot by means of a lie, pretending not to hear, refusing food, or by displaying an overly submissive attitude, such symptoms of adaptation, if carried into adulthood, may become diseases of adaptation—that is, they form part of a neurotic behavior.

All people have traumatic experiences. But apart from growing up, some people have been scarred more than others. Physically, we may still have scars from a cut, a fall, a burn, an accident, or a particularly severe punishment. We may remember the incident, or we may have forgotten it, but just as we say that there is a body or tissue memory, there certainly is a memory of the mind that buries unhappy events. Often, the more painful the event, the deeper we bury the memory of it.

I remember one patient who had forgotten entirely that he had spent some years in an orphanage when he was eleven years old immediately after the death of his mother. The entire episode had been so traumatic and painful to him that he denied its very existence. He had thrust it out of his mind so far that only with help was he able to recall it.

When in the absence of physical illness a person's pattern shows persistent nervous symptoms, we search for those traumatic experiences which had initially produced these symptoms. Whatever the trauma, the event itself—as well as the resulting responses—reveals a conflict which the individual had not been able to resolve and which consequently produced his unhappiness.

Such an individual retains a hypersensitivity or overreaction to situations similar to the original one. In his brain he has created a signal to which from now on he will react in a specific way similar to his original response. Later on in life, a certain attitude, a word, a gesture, a motion of rejection, in short, a signal, might produce a violent reaction far out of proportion to the incident itself, indeed a confusing occurence, bewildering to the people who become the target as well as the person himself, who is often unaware of the reasons for his undue arousal. In the hidden interplay of signal and response lies a man's often unwarranted outburst of fury at his wife—as a mother symbol—or an angry withdrawal from a boss as a father or mother symbol.

The young lawyer I have described earlier, whose domineering mother had turned out to be an obstacle to his happiness, reacted to an employment interviewer in precisely the same way he had become conditioned to react to his mother, namely with panic and a fear paralysis. Unconsciously it was not an employment person who interviewed him, but the image of his own rigid, critical mother. Though he had come to know this and wanted to change his behavior, he felt helpless and, after just a few minutes of such a session, his head would begin to swim and he would feel all tired out; then he would act, as he said, "like an idiot."

The physical symptoms the young lawyer experienced demonstrate well the relationship between his mind and body. They showed how deep-rooted his fears were, and how they affected his thought processes and his bodily functions. As much as he wanted to, he was not able to think freely for himself or to control his body's motoric restlessness. Rather, it was an automatic response to countless earlier events when he had to weigh each of his responses in terms of what his mother would think. His fear of her and her caustic criticism almost always paralyzed him, leaving him with an inner quiver or feelings of numbness. In due time he had become conditioned to react in such a specific way to anyone who represented authority.

It is true of all of us that the way we feel and think about ourselves becomes an integral part of our total being. We form an image about ourselves. This self-image plus the vast variety of responses we learn to develop is the result of our experiences, and are eventually built into us just as if they were part of our bones, nerves, and muscles. Each emotional experience, each interaction of events and thoughts, like each action of our lives, with its positive or negative reaction, leaves in our brain a memory which by repetition becomes strong and automatic. This is the basis of the stupendous work of Pavlov. After many years of experimentation and after he had established differences of behavior due to different environmental factors, he found that speech and thought form, in time, a direct route in the brain, like a short circuit. He called this a second signaling system of the conditioned reflex, since the response to speech and thought became as automatic as a natural reflex. They develop by repetition, hence the term "conditioned."

It was by an accidental occurence that Pavlov came to discover how extreme fear could wipe out a carefully established system of conditioning to a point that such an animal would lose its former responses and could be conditioned to develop new responses to new signals. His school then developed techniques, other than fear, which could be used positively for healing, by breaking neurotic habits; or the techniques could be used negatively for political brainwashing.

In 1924, the rising waters of the Neva River caused a great flood in Petrograd, later called Leningrad. It reached Pavlov's laboratories and flooded the kennels in which he had been keeping his conditioned dogs. The water rose dangerously close to the ceiling, and the dogs swam in utter terror, seeing no route of escape. At the last moment an attendant rescued the dogs, and, when Pavlov later examined them, he found that some of the animals had switched from a state of acute excitement to one of complete inhibition. Those observations puzzled him and led him to study, systematically, the causes which would have brought about the disappearance of the carefully established conditioned responses.

Pavlov came to the conclusion that when an overstimulation becomes so strong that it is threatening the functioning of the brain cells, inhibitory processes take place and bring to a halt their functioning in order to protect the cells from exhaustion or destruction. He called this process "protective inhibition." He found this protective act to be a regulatory device and a crucial factor in all struggles an animal must wage for its survival.

Later Pavlov and his school confirmed that a man's reflexes correspond exactly with those of a dog and that the act of protective inhibition leads not only to a decline of vitality, but is also the condition found in mental illness. In a remarkable paper the then eighty-year-old scientist published, he gave the reason why he, as a physiologist, had

43

undertaken the "excursion into the field of psychiatry." He said that not only had he been able to produce neuroses in his animals which were analogous to human psychosis, but that he knew their treatment.

Inhibition, he explained, plays the role of a guardian of the most reactive and irreplaceable cells of the organism—the cortical cells seated in the outer layers of the brain. Inhibition protects these cells against excessive tension at times when they have to meet extraordinary excitation. Protective inhibition secures them the necessary rest in the form of sleep. Sleep, after intense stimulation, spreads over both hemispheres of the brain. The brain cells recover.

The twilight state which exists between waking and sleeping is, according to Pavlov, similar to a real hypnotic state. It has differences in degree of inhibition and affects different areas of the brain. If a hypnotic state continues to exist for some length of time—a state called "chronic"—it produces symptoms of *apathy, dullness, immobility* and a *stereotyped behavior* which is a stubborn continuation and repetition of the same rigid movements. These are the very same symptoms which are found in human schizophrenia. This type of mental illness, according to Pavlov, is an existence in a kind of hypnotic state.

A nervous breakdown rarely occurs suddenly. It comes when an individual has helplessly or sometimes even willfully disregarded a series of warning signals and has exposed his brain cells to prolonged periods of excitation without relief. Such a person, often for reasons unknown to himself, had overburdened himself with responsibilities he could not meet and had remained in a state of conflict unable to make a decision. Or he had set unattainable standards for himself and considered himself a failure in discharging his responsibilities. At such times many a person may feel shame or guilt, or feel miserably inadequate and too discouraged to continue his struggle for life.

The period after a breakdown is often, as we stated, a time of inner revelation and reconstruction. In seclusion and in an atmosphere free from stress such a person may find himself and his place in the outside world. Often, we find that people who have had a breakdown come out of it not only stronger, but with greater determination and an ability to make decisions. They change. Confronted with an awareness of their mortality and man's most basic decision, like Hamlet's "to be or not to be," these people dare to examine the nature of their conflict and may then move toward resolving it by overcoming their wavering, wasteful indecision with regard to whatever it may be—a personal relationship, a marriage, their profession or a set of standards which they may discover are not really their own. Daring to cut their Gordian Knot or Knots, they may now be able to make a mature adjustment to a life in reality. In the deep inner struggle that takes place, one individual may be able to adjust to a more active or creative and hence happier life, while another, who is unable to make a final decision, remains confused and thereby prepares the ground for a next and even greater failure.

"Nervous breakdown" is a euphemistic, nonmedical term for either the onset of an emotional illness or for an acute psychotic episode.

The milder form of a breakdown—in the absence of a mental illness—can also teach us to apply the principle of protective inhibition. We must relieve the pressure of stress by getting out of an intolerable situation. We must take a rest or go on a vacation. Or better, by recognizing the cause or causes of our inner conflict, we must move to resolve it by fight or flight. Some destructive people, it seems, know what they are doing but the inner self-destructive impulses are stronger. They remain in a destructive relationship. They continue a self-destructive existence. Some people, driven by an awful curiosity or their obsessive-compulsive nature, feel compelled to go to the rim of the abyss before, like a hopeless alcoholic in a dim flash of awareness, they begin to pull themselves up by the bootstraps and start a new, creative life. Some people, who had been deprived of love, need constant excitement from without in order to overcome a feeling of deadness deep within. Certainly not before the individual is ready within himself to do this can there be an upswing.

Sometimes an episode of stress—a little breakdown—may not seem so severe. Almost everyone may go through a period when he cannot do his work well, when he is confused, wavers, forgets things, doesn't sleep well, quarrels easily or when he withdraws from people. At such a time we may need to be alone to recollect ourselves if there is enough inner strength. Otherwise, we should be aware of the warning signal and seek professional help so that we can be objective about ourselves and take stock of the situation which confronts us. At such a time we must come to recognize our specific Gordian Knot and dare to act. It may mean going through the agony of giving up the security of a home, or a job, or even a country, and to decide for an uncertain future. But as humans, in order to go on we must have beliefs and ideals and a sense of dignity. If the values within ourselves are destroyed by constant compromises and the meaning for our existence is chipped away, then a man becomes a shell, left with a sense of numbness in order not to feel self-hate, or he feels an inner lifelessness that is covered up by a facade of pretense. Happiness is lost. If it seems to exist, it is in a childish fairytale world of fantasy.

Many people destroy their chance for happiness because they fail to grow up.

A woman in her early fifties came to see me for what she called an annoying and puzzling problem. She experienced an uncontrollable tiredness, but only,—and this mystified her—when, in the performance of her work, she had to meet a new client. Away from business, at home, or with friends, she said she felt fine. With some sense of humor she said that just at those very moments when she had to be particularly brilliant and imaginative she felt a leaden heaviness in her eyelids which, no matter how hard she fought their drooping, drew together as if commanded to do so by a hypnotist. "There must be some physical reason for this," she said, "perhaps a vitamin deficiency or some dreadful anemia."

The patient—let us call her Nancy Palmer—was a former radio commentator who, with a young woman partner, was establishing a public relations business in New York City. She had excellent contacts and all seemed to go well until she had to meet a number of executives to discuss her ideas and promotional strategy. Then the embarrassing symptom of falling asleep occurred. For about a year she had been feeling a marked decline in her vitality. She had consulted a doctor who explained that this lack of energy was due to low blood pressure and low blood sugar. She had been given a series of injections and medication. At first there was an immediate improvement, but after a few months she began to feel the same as before and gave up taking her pills and the injections.

Since the patient seemed so convinced that she had some

mysterious illness, I had her take new tests which showed that she was not anemic, that her blood-sugar level was not low, and that no other physical deficiency could be detected. In answer to my question as to what she thought might have been causing her low physical feelings and the blue moods, she said that she found herself pondering about this, for she knew of no reason why she should feel so badly at a time when a really great success in business seemed imminent. She had fought very hard for this chance, and now, when it was about to fall into her lap, these disturbing symptoms had appeared threatening to destroy her efforts. She had lived in California, but after her mother's death had given up her home and job to come East. "Perhaps," she said, "it is the change of climate."

She revealed that she had never been close to anyone except her mother. She insisted that she had had a happy childhood, and that throughout her life she had been a very happy and a very lucky person until her mother's death about two years before. She had loved her mother with profound devotion. She spoke of her earlier memories waiting for her mother to come home from work. She said she learned later that her father had left the family one day and never returned, and that she had never seen him. She did not know that this incident had deepened in her an enormous distrust of men and that she had never overcome a bitter sense of rejection. She remembered her dreadful feelings of anxiety every morning when her mother left, and still recalls the apprehensive and long and lonely hours waiting for her return.

A child of a broken home, she had lived with her mother and an aunt. Her mother was employed. Her aunt kept house. The child resented the aunt's discipline and continuous criticism. She felt the aunt hated her and punished her disloyal father in her, and the child in turn hated the aunt. Only with her mother did she feel safe, and therefore she longed for her protection and companionship, only to find that she was shunted aside. The mother, always tired and frustrated, had little time for the child. The child's mind, anguished and bewildered, distorted the unbearable reality, imagining that her mother loved her 'darling little girl.' Long childhood hours were spent dreaming of the days to come when she could prove to her mother by some great achievement how worthy she was of mother's love and that mother then would send her aunt away and both would live together happily ever after.

In time it came about. The aunt died. The girl grew into a beautiful young woman who was herself employed, and acquired a name in her field, liked and admired by many. It gave her pleasure to support her mother, who then retired. The girl's career involved much socializing. This was a period of happy companionship between mother and daughter, the mother now depending on the daughter not only for her support, but to be amused by the daughter's description of the successes during her days and the social events at night. The depth of the neurotic involvement of this relationship became evident at the time her mother died. While a parent's death is always a trauma, it was excessively so in this case. The daughter had emotionally remained a little girl. She had not built a life of her own and with her one interest or meaning of life—her mother—gone, she lost her incentive to perform. She had no one to prove herself to, and, in a moment of dejection, she gave up her radio career entirely. She disposed of the business she had built, gave it to her associates and moved thousands of miles away to New York City. There, in time, she formed a partnership with a young woman and began to develop what promised to be a successful public relations agency. Then her health problem occurred and threatened her with a discontinuation of the partnership.

It was quite evident that our patient's relationship with her mother had been one of abnormal interdependence. It was neurotic because the involvement was so very excessive and contrary to a normal development, which has the aim for a growing child to gain freedom and independence. Here we had no freedom and absolute dependency. Our patient, starting as a child and continuing later as a growing girl, clung more and more to her mother for security. This thwarted her emotional maturity and created one of the most destructively neurotic states called "symbiosis," a Greek term for "a life together". Actually, what is meant by symbiosis is a parasitic interrelationship, each person feeding on the other, as the fetus, fed and carried by the mother, also gives the mother a meaning for her existence.

Having remained a passive dependent personality, she was motivated by one great desire—to please her mother to a point of complete submission to her. Any anger was severely

48

repressed or transferred to her aunt or some aunt substitute. Her inability to cut her Gordian Knot had not allowed this woman to move toward independence. Therefore, after her mother's death, she felt lost and without direction.

During her fourth visit to me, she said that she had made a strange discovery. While lunching with her partner and two other women, she suddenly turned white and became panicky when one of the other women indicated how much she would like to have the partner as an associate. The very suggestion threw my patient into a state of panic and of intense jealousy for fear of losing her partner. She now dimly realized how much her partner had taken the place of her mother. Losing her partner meant losing her mother all over again, and with it, the new, fragile incentive for a productive life. This discovery disturbed her greatly, for it pointed out to her how childishly dependent on her partner she had become while believing herself to be an independent self-reliant woman and in control of the business relationship.

Living alone, the woman further realized that she had no one with whom to discuss her personal thoughts and problems and it was frightening for her to discover how empty her life was. She was not really interested in her business. She wanted a mother substitute. The incident at the luncheon made her distressingly aware of her helplessness and that she could not work alone. In retrospect, thinking back to her earlier years, she suddenly realized that her dates with young men and all the other aspects of her social life had not been for her own pleasure and progress but meant to gain material which she used to amuse her mother who was enjoying her every belittling of men so that both could heartily laugh together at the men's insecure or foolish behavior. Nancy was in a trap. She could not live without her mother, and she could not bring her mother back to life. She had stated initially that she felt fatigued at critical moments and that she was not functioning properly. It was evident now that she had been in the throes of indecision all her life. Her outwardly efficient functioning and success in a career was possible because no independent decision had ever been asked of her. She had been in a habit of discussing every problem with her mother. During her professional interviews, she conducted herself as a well-conditioned, well-trained person, strictly conforming and submitting to the rules of a boss or a network or an authority just as she had conformed to the rules of her own mother. Like a toy poodle, well groomed, attractive, pleasant, she was liked because she pleased everybody and was a threat to no one.

Her falling asleep at the crucial moments when she had to be alert to secure her livelihood indicated that she could not or did not want to cope with a life of reality. What she wanted was to turn her partner into her mother. This created tensions because the younger woman resisted the personal turn their business meetings seemed to take. Nancy Palmer became increasingly more tense as her partner became more impatient. Unable to "function," that is to follow her neurotic pattern, caused her to withdraw emotionally. The harder she tried to impress her younger partner and the less the younger partner responded, the greater Nancy's feelings of failure and panic. To invoke the principle of protective inhibition—falling asleep during a business session—meant a desparate need to get out of a battle that was not gratifying. Symbolically it was not a gesture of a temporary cease fire and then to take up the battle again with more strength but to give up in order to be reunitèd with her mother—that is to die.

When an animal is ready to die it stops eating. The same with man, not all men of course, but with the many who are tired all the time, who are too nervous to eat and who unconsciously aim to ruin their job, thereby destroying their livelihood. This is precisely what this woman was doing.

Nancy Palmer resisted facing the reality of her position for a long time. Her intelligence and her final admission how miserable she really felt deep within herself, gave her enough motivation to go on with her therapy.

Practically, the only one road open to prevent a serious breakdown and her unconscious wish to die was to break the personal relationship between the two partners without destroying their business. A compromise formula could be found by Nancy moving back to California and her younger partner staying in New York, and it took a considerable period of time for the older woman to give up her neurotic fantasies so that she and her younger partner could meet in a more relaxed and businesslike fashion. The fruitful coexistence of these two people was made possible by the older woman's act of eventually cutting her Gordian Knot. True enough, it was done with great reluctance but Nancy

Palmer recognized the inevitability of accepting herself as an adult who had to stand on her own two feet without the need for an imaginary supportive mother figure.

Coming back to the man with the alleged heart attack, he could admit that he had been a deeply troubled man for a long time. He had tried very hard to play the game right in a society which he found confusing and full of contradictions. He had anglicized his name to conceal his Jewish background. During World War II he was trying hard to be a courageous fighter pilot in the Air Force who could never allow himself to show fear. After the war he had married a gentile woman, a stunning actress, and moved into an upper middle class suburban community. All seemed to go well at first but friction developed at home. He could never relax, his wife never ceased to be discontented because she had failed in her career as an actress and had sought security in a marriage.

As a man, my patient lacked the security to cope with his dissatisfied wife. Sexually she rejected him and kept on telling him just to leave her alone and to get his dirty sex somewhere else. And so the frustration at home and the disappointment in business had created unbearable tensions which his emotional personality could not withstand. He broke down.

He was not an enthusiastic patient but he realized that he was in need of help and he respected the clarification he was gaining. After a year and a half he left. All seemed to go better. Several years later he returned for about two consultations only. He was a changed man. He had made an enormous success in business. He had a mistress who thought that he was the greatest lover ever born. Life at home was pleasant. The children who had difficulties had become better adjusted after a school psychologist had a number of sessions with their mother. The man's breakdown had become the turning point of his life. He began to experience a sense of happiness he had never had before.

This man, or Nancy Palmer, or the young lawyer or all the people who wait in thousands of doctors' offices—or the many more people who don't even dare to go to see a doctor—they all have one thing in common: a need to be freed from an illness of unhappiness. They are in conflict and suffer pain which is not of the body and which they therefore don't understand. These people are aware that life is passing them by, yet they feel helpless to grab a part of the mystical vital force other people seem to possess and which is painfully demonstrated to them by the shrieking laughter of children at play, a young couple out on a date, a young family at a ball-play, an old couple walking along a street holding hands as they have done for decades—all expressions of the inner joy we call happiness.

To the many unhappy people, Pavlov's concept of protective inhibition gives us a scientific explanation of what happens to the highly sensitive cortical cells in the outer layers of the brain when unrelieved pressure and stress and fear begin to depress their normal functioning and when a state of growing inhibition paralyzes their freedom of action. When in these people the first symptoms of apathy, dullness, immobility and stereotyped movements appear, it is evident that they have been moving toward a disorganized condition we call a nervous breakdown.

But before people experience any or all of these classical symptoms they go as a rule through periods of unhappiness. These people, or anyone who wishes to stay well must therefore search for the conflict that makes him unhappy and that is slowly breaking him down. Unhappy people must ask themselves, what is their Gordian Knot? Why have they not been able first to recognize and then to cut their Knot? What are the fears which keep these unfortunate people from taking the action which will lead them out of their conflict, an action which at a moment of clarity they know they must take if they—or for that matter anyone in conflict must take who truly desires a life of happiness.

4.

Why Are Some More NEUROTIC than Others?

THE INCIDENT OF THE NEVA FLOOD LED PAVLOV TO OBSERVE that when stress or panic threatened to damage the cortical cells of the brain a state of *protective inhibition* brought the activity of these cells to a stop. This, Pavlov theorized, was necessary to allow time for repair action and recovery from the damaging effect of exhaustion resulting from an extreme expenditure of energy. Though the dogs trapped in their kennels continued to go through the motions of swimming, there was a point when their actions became mechanical and apathetic, almost torpid. They seemed to have reached a point of indifference as to whether to keep on swimming or stop. In view of studies done in this country several years ago, the behavior of the dogs may be seen in a significant new light. Curt P. Richter, professor of psychobiology at Johns Hopkins Medical School, working with wild Norwegian rats, had found that these vigorous animals when trapped beyond hope of escape would give up and drown. Richter came to the conclusion that "rats as well as human beings die from a reaction of hopelessness."

Pavlov's dogs obviously had not given up hope. They were numbed, however, to a point where they lost their identity, for the patterns of response which had been so carefully built into them by Pavlov's experiments had vanished as if they had been totally erased.

Pavlov discovered, however, that not all the dogs responded to the experience to the same extent. Some kept their conditioned responses longer than others. He concluded that some of the dogs were of a stronger and others of a weaker constitution, and that they could be divided into two groups: one type, the stronger, he described as lively and excitatory; the other he called weak and inhibitory. He then conducted experiments which confirmed his assumption.

Pavlov's famous experiment with the salivating dog had long before already demonstrated the conditioned reflex. In this experiment, Pavlov rang a bell at the same time that he presented food to the dog. When the dog saw his food, his salivary glands responded and his mouth "watered." This was repeated over and over until the day came when Pavlov merely rang the bell. Though no food was there, the salivary glands responded to the signal in exactly the same manner, producing exactly the same amount of gastric juice as if meat had been presented. Pavlov called this a conditioned reflex, since the response was now as automatic as a natural reflex. The characteristic of a reflex, conditioned or natural, is that its response to a stimulus is *involuntary;* that is, it is not subject to the conscious will. Also, similar to the action of the salivary glands, other reflexes in human and animal conduct could be conditioned.

On my visit to the renowned Pavlov Institute at Koltushi near Leningrad, I learned about another of the many experiments Pavlov had conducted. Taking eight puppies from the same litter, he kept four in solitary confinement for a period of two years, while he allowed the other four to live the normal existence of puppies. At the end of the two-year period, a marked difference of behavior could be observed. The isolated puppies were timid, weak, inhibited creatures, whereas the other four were normal, healthy, lively dogs. Since all eight puppies were from the same litter, these differences in personality were not likely to be hereditary, but the result of factors of their environment. In still further experiments Pavlov was able to show that later training could produce further differences in personality.

A weak, timid dog could by conditioning be made in time to seem like an extrovert. Yet, to the discerning eye, a difference was still evident. In their outward behavior timid dogs were never quite as bold as their brothers. However, the real difference was not apparent until a moment of crisis. A sudden noise, a gun shot, or the explosion of a firecracker near one of the dogs would cause a timid animal to revert to his basic type. He would tremble, make a dash for a hiding place, or cringe along a wall in search of security. The strong and lively dogs might merely look around to see what had caused the noise, or a hunting dog would take his cue.

Doctors have known for a long time that people portray individual differences of behavior and that their human patients develop personality traits very much like those Pavlov observed in his dogs. Hippocrates, called the "father of medicine," made a classification of personality types which, if less scientific than Pavlov's, is nevertheless based on the same observation of human nature. It was so useful that generation after generation of physicians upheld his theory through medieval times and almost until the beginnings of modern science. Hippocrates theorized that there are four fluids in the body and a tendency of one of these to predominate governs the personality or temperament of the person. The four fluids in the body were yellow bile, making the typical choleric or angry man; red blood, making the sanguine or cheerful, adaptable man; phlegm, making the phlegmatic or stolid man; and black bile, causing a melancholy temperament.

Pavlov knew that these fluids had no causal relationship with the effects Hippocrates had seen in his patients. But Pavlov did know from observations confirmed by experiments that dogs and people tend to develop either a positive or negative type of personality, either an aggressive or inhibited behavior. Various names have been given by the many physicians who have made similar observations. Jung spoke of extroverts or introverts, Karen Horney, the American psychiatrist, of people moving "against" (hostile behavior), "toward" (friendly-adjusted behavior), and "away" from people (withdrawal).

Pavlov further defined his types into four categories: the strong excitatory-aggressive; the lively-controlled aggressive; the calm, imperturbable; and the weak, inhibitory-withdrawn type. I find it useful to call these personality types the hostile-aggressive, the adjusted, the passive-dependent, and the withdrawn-inhibited. While they correspond, as can be seen, to Hippocrates' choleric, sanguine, phlegmatic, and melancholic temperaments, all that really matters, from the point of a healthy and happy pursuit of life, is whether our basic attitude is positive—that is, life-affirming—or basically negative and life-denying, for it is this latter orientation which tends to lead to mentally depressed states and unhappiness due to over-inhibition. From a point of understanding disturbed people and treating them, it is helpful to distinguish a hostile-aggressive from a passive-dependent or withdrawn, regressive behavior. (The adjusted type makes up a rather small bulk of patients only.)

Evaluating personalities, one must keep in mind the true responses of people to situations and not be deceived by a pseudo-friendliness in the hostile or a pseudo-aggression in the passive individual.

One of my patients may serve as an example of his peculiar type of personality and how he could not break out of the rigid circumstance of his conditioning. He made his first visit to my office on the urging of his wife. She had made this consultation a birthday present to him. She had felt powerless, frustrated, and miserably unhappy watching her husband ruining his professional life, as well as his health, while she felt herself cracking up. The man had come with reluctance, but with more curiosity than annoyance. Our first interview began as a kind of fencing match. He answered questions, but volunteered no information, and I noted certain subtle provocations on his part which were met on mine by strenuous efforts, which must have been equally obvious, to disregard them. These provocations gave me the first clues about my patient's temperament.

He was in his middle fifties, energetic, and, on the surface, jovial. But he had an obviously low threshold of tolerance and exploded quickly when antagonized. I had been warned by his wife that this might be fatal to any successful treatment, and I was careful not to provoke him.

However, it was soon possible for me to bring the subject of irritability into our conversation. He admitted that he was aware of his vile temper, but he was fatalistic about it. He maintained that it was not so very serious. In any case, he considered it part of his nature and that nothing could be done about it. "Not exploding." he said, "would make me feel worse."

This is a point on which all psychologists, whether Freudian or Pavlovian, agree; namely, that repression or inhibition is always unhealthy. Yet, while this is basically true, civilization would be impossible without a great deal of repression of instinctual drives. What psychology is trying to do therefore is to reduce the excess of it, to make the necessary repression understandable and bearable, but not to remove it completely, since without a certain degree of repression an organized society would be unthinkable, and the comparative peace and security we as individuals enjoy would be downright impossible. A total rejection of repression would mean a return to jungle law.

My patient's lack of self-control had cost him not only his harmonious relationship with his wife, but serious setbacks in his career as a lawyer. He tried to justify his conduct on the grounds of principle. He excused his conduct by saying that when he was provoked by injustice he tended to flare into a rage over which he had no control. "There is a great deal of injustice in this world," he said, "and it will only grow stronger unless it is vigorously opposed. A man must have principle if he wants to retain self-respect. Fighting for a principle may get one into a lot of trouble, but losing self-respect is the end and about the worst thing that can happen to a man."

Almost the worst. Losing his self-control had lost this man his first career. Many violent clashes with the judge led to repeated warnings that he would be held in contempt of court, but he continued to disregard these warnings and this eventually led to his permanent disbarment. He was forced to turn to a career as a tax adviser.

As our interview proceeded, I encouraged him to tell me something of his early history. A reference to his father, to whom he referred as "the old man" and for whom he claimed to have had a great deal of respect, gave me an important clue. He described his father's temper, and, admitted that he had always feared it. He said that the old man's voice alone could stir his blood. It became apparent that he had been a dutiful, exemplary, obedient son—a status he had achieved only by repressing his own anger, which continued to simmer within him to appear later in ever-explosive rebellion. He had decided right then that later in life no one would ever bully him or talk down to him or push him around.

Apparently, his father's temper had served him as a model, and the pattern of poor self-control had established itself early in his life and grown stronger through repetition. When he came to see me, the need to resist his father had long since passed, because his father had not been living for many years. But his conditioning to overreact to any symbol of authority remained, be it a judge, a police officer or a doctor. Through his established pattern of behavior, he was quick to fight with anyone who crossed him, including his wife. He was quite unaware of the reasons for his conduct. He tried to justify it and excuse it without knowing that underneath these pretensions there was a neurotic tendency to quarrel. He did not know that he was motivated by a militant need to oppose any type of rebellion. "It is my Irish blood," he said excusingly. He could not even admit to himself that he was an unhappy person, although his over-aggressive conduct had ruined his first career and threatened to do the same to his second career.

This man is a representative of the hostile-agressive type of personality. His neurosis does not in itself make him unhappy, for, by his explosions, he gets rid of the unbearable tensions from his internal conflicts. At the same time, unfortunately, he created a conflict with some external obstacle, like the judge, and thereby makes trouble for himself even if he rationalizes that he is acting in the cause of justice.

As an example of the passive-dependent personality, let us briefly return to Nancy Palmer, the engaging lady who fell asleep when she was about to meet her important clients. This symptom, we explained to be an act of protective inhibition.

She grew up without the love and guidance of a father and consequently had no chance to develop a clear image of what an ideal male was like. Standing at the window for hours waiting for her mother could not create in her a sense of security but rather apprehension and anxiety. So boundless was her need for love and protection that she accepted her mother unconditionally thereby squashing anger and resentment (except for her aunt) but also squashing any drive for independence. This made her a passive dependent personality. And the sum of the depressing experiences conditioned her to move in only one direction, to win approval from all people in authority in order to be loved.

Having knitted the ties with her mother as closely as she did, Nancy had become a prisoner who lived in an ivory tower with her mother. This unhealthy state of co-existence led to another neurotic sense of fulfillment. By supporting her mother and also having emulated her personality, Nancy symbolically lived out the role of being her mother's mother and being as protective as if her mother were her child.

This was pleasurable and gave her life meaning until her mother died and she moved to New York. Of course, Nancy did not know that she took her neurotic personality structure with her to New York, where she felt like a satellite in desperate search of a lost planet. She used her brilliance and talents to knit her partner to her and to turn her into a mother-substitute.

It was the healthy resistance of the young woman who felt the obscure emotional interplay and fought it vigorously. The young woman respected the talents of her older partner and enjoyed the friendship but rejected this friendship being turned into a sick relationship, which made it possible for them to stay in business.

There is a healthy need people have for a relationship with people who can satisfy their own dependency needs. The difference in Nancy Palmer's case was only one of degree, not of kind. To deny dependency needs in oneself, out of the fear of being controlled, can cause people to become immensely lonely and unhappy. It can cause withdrawal to a point where they become distant and isolated, feeling misunderstood and out of place in a confusing and estranged, vast world.

Protection of the ego, which requires a certain amount of self-esteem, is an absolute necessity in enduring life, and life, being what it is, confronts the ego with threats of diminishment or injury all the time. The reaction to these threats is either to annihilate them, which is fight, or to remove ourselves from the firing line, which is flight. Some people, like the lawyer I described earlier, are quick on the trigger and launch a counterattack at the slightest rustle of danger; some are so excitable that they launch a preventive attack like a preventive war, before the danger has even become a reality.

And there are others who do exactly the opposite. At the first hint of danger they retire to the safety of their fort, lift the drawbridge, lower the portcullis, and hide as far away as possible from the battle where they live in fright.

The causes of these responses are as numerous as the millions of signals we develop in the course of our growing up. The child observes and emulates his parents. Anger provokes anger and fear provokes fear. Initial success, when the growing child dares to assert himself, is the beginning of a trend, but so is initial failure. If the first response to a threat to the ego happens to be a counterattack, because this was the example in the home environment, and if it has proven successful, then the next response is also likely to be a counterattack, since success encourages repetition. But if the first attack was a failure and resulted in defeat, then different tactics are likely to be tried the next time the ego is threatened. Retreat to safety may then become the watchword in order to avoid humiliation, criticism or defeat. With each repetition of similar tactics, the tendency becomes a stronger, more permanent part of the behavior of the individual.

In the course of life a continuation of defeats may cause the defenses to grow so thin that one last straw may effect a breakdown. If such a person has a psychotic personality structure—and we are at this time still not clear how much in our makeup is genetic, chemical, and environmental—which, we may add, can be so well disguised that many psychotic personalities are considered normal especially when they possess a brilliant intellect that helps to conceal a lingering mental illness. With such a person a sudden event can cause an eruption into a full-fledged, psychotic episode. Such an event in the eyes of the world may be of minor importance, but to the individual himself may be the signal powerful enough to set off a chain reaction.

An example of this is a woman who found life so confusing and her anguish and repressed rage so immense, that one last minor rejection caused her to suffer an acute psychotic episode in which she offered to kill me, not because she was motivated by a need to hurt me, but because of her urgent need to seek relief from her own intolerable tensions. Life appeared to her as one inescapable prison and was baffling to her wherever she turned. No undertaking of hers was gratifying, no efforts successful, whether in marriage or employment, in making a literary career for herself or her volunteer charity work. Wherever she tried she experienced failure, and her self-hate had reached a point that she could not stand any longer. In her personal restricted life she was lonely, ill, forlorn and depressed. Her last money was gone. It was a wonder that she carried on the fight and was still willing to live at all, since her situation was desperate, and her future seemed hopeless.

She was about forty, timid, tired, frail, almost ethereal in appearance. I had been treating her for a variety of symptoms due to her underlying depression on and off for more than a year, and I knew some of the details of her life.

One day she kept an appointment with me and, as I greeted her in my usual manner, I noticed something different about her—an appearance of strain so great that she trembled in her effort to keep control of herself. I asked her to sit down, but she remained standing, staring at me.

"No" she said in a low, soft voice. "I can't, because now . . . I must kill you." Startled, I looked at her pocketbook, wondering if it contained a weapon, .wondering what step she might take next. I knew that I had to win time and that I had to keep her talking. By the way she kept staring at me with strange, calculating, determined eyes, I knew she was mad. Trying to appear calm, I sat down and asked her, in as gentle a voice as I could manage, "What is the matter? Why don't you just sit down and tell me. Why do you want to kill me?" She remained standing. "Because it is easier to kill you than someone else," she said, "and I must kill someone . . . now." But as she said this I noticed the beginning of a change. The rigidity in her face eased, and she said, "You have done me no harm. You were nice, but I can't contain an urge to kill somebody." She shook her head as if shaking herself out of a trance. "And I know I'm going to do it. I don't know how long I can control this terrible feeling I have. Help me," she whispered. "I came to you for help. I don't want to do it, but I'm going to." At this point she sat down, and I knew for a moment the crisis—my crisis—was over, not hers.

During the preceding year I had learned much about what had brought her to this state. She had been a frail, sickly child, and, because of her inability to engage in activities with other children, had indulged in a fantasy life from a very early period. Fantasy is a means of escape all children indulge in. In her case, the indulgence was carried to an extent where the fantasy became more gratifying than reality.

In adolescence her unacceptance of reality continued. At this time she wrote poetry and hoped one day that she might be a famous poet. It is characteristic of persons in this condition that they set extremely high and almost unattainable standards for themselves. These are meant to compensate for and to dispel all the feelings of inadequacy, and to prove one day to the world their worth.

As my patient grew older, her health continued poor. She tended to blame her lack of success in the many enterprises in her life on her poor physical health and shaky nerves. As long as she could remember she had had spells of weakness and melancholia. She married, but this venture ended in miserable failure, a separation. She did not even accept support from her former husband, because she felt she had failed him.

She had taken all kinds of temporary jobs to support herself, but felt that she had never been truly successful in any of them. In her search for some solution for her problem of unhappiness, she undertook psychoanalytic treatment and continued for seven years. Hopeful of a cure, she made enormous personal sacrifices, working long hours at uncongenial jobs to pay for this treatment, and while she said that it had helped to some degree she admitted that she had not been really able to apply in her life what she theoretically knew she should do.

During this time she undertook to continue her literary career by writing a novel, but this was rejected in turn by several publishers, with unsympathetic criticisms. Is it any wonder that such a person felt that she was on the verge of a complete breakdown?

Her writing, poetry and the novel, was an extension of her life of fantasy. It was her attempt to make reality fit her pattern, instead of doing what a healthy person would do to adapt herself to reality. This is not to say that there is anything wrong with writing poetry or novels. This may often be very good therapy. What is wrong is to expect the world to pay any attention to poetry or writing if it is written for the neurotic need or pleasure of the individual. Again, a healthy person would be able to understand and accept such writing or artistic work to satisfy one's own narcissism.

In my patient's case, her vivid fantasy life became a conditioned escape mechanism. Her fantasies began in early childhood as a gratifying flight from a bewildering reality, and, as they continued, their retarding effect on the growth of her emotional personality increased. At the same time, however, she could not fail to be aware of her separation and estrangement from reality. As the demands of reality to become a responsible woman increased, the conflict between escaping and assuming mature responsibilities became more intense, finally causing a flare-up of her mental disorder, with an increasing disintegration of her personality.

All of us continue to have a certain fantasy life as long as we may live, and the relationship of this life to reality may be considered as an index of sanity. The normal person is easily able to distinguish between what is fantasy and what is real. There is sometimes no easy, absolute dividing line between normal and abnormal, or sane and insane, but where reality becomes increasingly difficult to pursue, there the degree of sanity decreases.

My patient's frailty and separation from other children as a youngster had developed a tendency in her to be timid and withdrawn. Her attempts at various times over the years to break this pattern of habit were unsuccessful, because they were not understood and because there was no one to help her.

Like many sick people, she hoped by one giant step to reach the exalted position that her fantasy reassured her she deserved. She had attempted the impossible and thereby invited defeat, which in turn served to confirm her belief that she should withdraw from a world she did not understand or that did not understand her. In time this became a personality pattern which we can recognize as weak-inhibitory or regressive. This kind of personality withdraws into itself behind a wall which remains as an obstacle between them and other people, between such a person's inner and the outer world, and makes it difficult or impossible to relate to others on a human and emotional level. Besides the difficulty to communicate feelings these people can as a rule not make decisions or perform almost any but the most routine, overt acts. As social beings they feel isolated, and, while they may have a natural desire of self and the assertion of their ego, this desire is blocked by their inhibition. The tensions from such conflict demand an outlet.

With drugs and reassurance this woman had been helped in the past to a point where in recent weeks she had felt encouraged enough to apply for volunteer nursing duty at a city hospital in order to do something useful. Having been accepted, she had been given assignments in a children's ward. But, very shortly before the visit which I have just described, where she threatened me, she had had an unfortunate experience.

In the children's ward was a small, deprived, non-

English-speaking boy, whose rigid, frightened expression attracted her sympathies. Not feeling threatened, she dared to show feelings. She spoke to him kindly, patiently, told him how beautiful he was and how lovable. As he watched her and heard her talk, he began to smile. His rigidity relaxed and she felt that she had helped him. She enjoyed her work that day very much.

When she returned the next afternoon, the president of the woman's club in charge of the volunteer operation expressed pleasure with her work but advised, in a very kind manner, that "the ladies who do this work must not give of themselves too much. They must not overtire themselves. Remember, this is volunteer work."

My patient was so discouraged by a remark she did not understand and considered to be a criticism that she could not return to the children's ward. "There is no sense in returning," she explained. "How can you help a frightened child without giving it every comfort and warmth?"

She took the president's words as a rejection, which is a characteristic of the weak-inhibitory personality, since rejection has helped to shape this type of personality structure in the first place and since these people interpret everything short of praise as a personal rejection. But, although she outwardly accepted the criticism, it shook her up. She had identified with the child. Her ego fought hard against her repressed anger but was too fragmented and weak to stem the rising tide of rage. Her tensions had become unmanageable and her control began to break.

Sometimes the imagined world, remote and peaceful, may give a person his only chance for physical survival. Sometimes the person who seeks it withdraws into it so far that he becomes unaffected by what goes on around him. He then is unapproachable by the members of his family, his friends, and those who try to reach him by the language of the real world. Sometimes the withdrawal is into a world of malice, danger, suspicion, and plotting, and the person in it seeks revenge for his suffering, even if this is only a wanton striking out against anyone nearby; then we have an unrestrained killer running amuck. Some of these dynamics had taken place in my patient, who dimly knew that she was about to lose herself in a blind striking out against the world that she believed had so unjustly tormented her.

Fortunately, in this case—and fortunately for me—she had

not yet completely lost touch with the tangible world around her. Even as she threatened, the complications of her bizarre actions came through to her, and she broke down and begged for someone to take care of her or to commit her to an institution where she could be helped.

This was not the time to explain to her the attitude of the woman's club president or to scold it. The tolerance of my patient had reached its limit. I felt her eyes watching my moves with undeterred attention, as I dialed Bellevue Hospital to arrange for her admittance. Only after I had written a note for the admitting office did she relax for a moment. She realized that soon she would be safe. She was admitted and consequently sent to a state mental hospital. What had saved the situation—and myself, I may add—at a moment when this woman could not control her rising agitation was the one thin line of communication left, and, since she trusted me, it could be used on her behalf and those of the people around her. The great difficulty in many similar cases is that the patient has no one to turn to or has so completely lost touch with reality that communication becomes impossible, and that violence is turned against other people, and then against oneself. And yet, underneath this violence, there is a poor, lost deprived human being, begging for one word of kindness, trying to understand the rules of a bewildering world of reality.

It is to the credit of our century that the growing understanding of what goes on in the dark inner world of a sick person has brought into existence the preventive measures of mental health programs by which trained personnel try to reach desperate human beings before they break, before they destroy, and in time so that they can be helped. But unless these people are encouraged to ask for help and unless more help is available for them, tragedies will happen. A most deplorable mistake which prevents some from seeking help in time is that they have been brought up with the notion that asking for help is a sign of weakness, while not asking for help is a sign of strength, a "proper" attitude, and a matter of individual pride.

The adjusted personality, the fourth of Pavlov's types, is what most people desire but which they often don't know how to attain. And yet we have in us the elements to love, to create, and to give, as well as the feelings of violence, hostility, envy, jealousy, dependency, and inhibition. Sur-

65

vival means keeping our lives in balance, but happiness—a step beyond survival—demands an understanding of the extent of the heterogeneous forces within us and the inter-dynamic play of our emotional life. Towards that goal self-understanding is a first unavoidable step.

5.

To MAKE or
BREAK a Habit

THE TIME IS NEW YEAR'S EVE, THE PLACE A NOISY PARTY, THE drama that of a pensive, keenly introspective man reviewing his past failures and scanning the prospects of his future. "I must change things," he mumbles. "After tomorrow I'm going to take a good firm grip on myself. I'm going to stop wasting my time. I can do it. I can start with cutting out that second highball and, of course, these filthy cigarettes. I really don't need them. I can get up a bit earlier and walk part of the way to my office. No more nonsense like these idiotic television programs at night. It's going to be a life of decision and action." Pleased with this decision he relaxes and takes a last drink. After all, it's New Year's Eve. The next morning he allows himself a day of grace to sleep late. But the morning after he keeps to his resolve. He is happy. The following morning he oversleeps. There is no time for his walk, and by the third day he knows that nothing has changed.

"Habit," he may say, somewhat crushed, and accuse himself of having no character. Yet, this accusation is neither true nor fair. He may possess character, by which he meant self-control but may not really want another life. If he truly wanted to change, his complaint would be that he had not given himself enough time to recondition his reflexes. He was a victim of the magnetic power of habit.

The difficulty generally is that people think in terms of will power rather than to consider the power of the established pattern of their conditioned reflexes and learn to change those.

Likes and dislikes, attitudes and idiosyncrasies and certainly the varied scale of emotional responses are reflexes which operate like our bodily functions—similar to the blinking of our eyes when we are suddenly confronted by the threat of a moving object, or our blushing when we feel embarrassed, or the pounding of our heart or the breaking out in perspiration when we are suddenly frightened. Even our intellectual attitudes toward the political and social issues of our time are under their sway. And these reflexes are also conditioned and as automatic as the secretions of our glands or the functions of our organs and muscles. By repetition of the same associations over and over they become involuntary and an integral part of our personality. Let us consider the case of a boy who believes he loves his father whom he has heard advocating isolationism as a good thing for the United States. The boy grows up to be an isolationist, not because he had been convinced by his father's arguments or because he has reached the same conclusion independently, but because the love of his father and the advocacy of isolationism have become associated in his mind, and because repetition of this association has made the idea a part of him—or a conditioned reflex. And thus we form principles ranging from tolerant, liberal ideas to ultraconservative dogmatic or even fanatical beliefs.

Success encourages repetition, failure discourages it. Therefore, by their very repetition successes usually become part of our personality as a conditioned reflex; of course, the same process operates in reverse with failure. If we want to establish a habit we must repeat the action over and over until it becomes an automatic process; the same with thought. That is, one can even condition one's own thoughts to evoke a specific response, as we shall point out later. Patient and consistent repetition will accomplish a desired result. It is the basis of any training, be it a man or a puppy dog.

To break a habit, repetition is also the key. Each time the habit suggests itself it must be resisted, and each time it is successfully resisted the habit becomes weaker and the resistance thereafter easier. But since a conditioned reflex is not a conscious action and often manifests itself before we are aware of it, we must learn to be on guard. We must become aware of our rising feelings and be prepared to substitute a new action for the old one, since a stimulus has set in motion a chain reaction which requires release of the mobilized energy.

Habits, whether of mind or action, are developed reflexes, and the behavior of a personality can be considered to be the sum of our conditioned reflexes. If we understand this we understand why we so often, like the man on New Year's Eve, fail to carry through our resolutions. By the same token, we can understand what we must do if we really want to make a resolution successful.

In explaining himself to an interviewer, the young lawyer described in Chapter 1 unconsciously saw, not the interviewer, but his mother, to whom, since earliest childhood, he had so often and so unsuccessfully tried to explain himself. Her criticism and her appraisal of him had never been warm and sympathetic, but cold and sharp, and he therefore developed the habit of reacting with fear and terror to these sessions with her before he even heard her comments. The interviewer, as a symbol of power, caused in him an identical response. His behavior was merely a conditioned reflex mechanism operating automatically. He had learned to think out his problems carefully, but his many attempts to approach a situation differently, and with courageous and positive thoughts, crumbled away in the presence of a symbol of authority. Any such attempt at behaving differently was like fumbling with the last link of a chain, for the powerful responses of fear and inhibition like an electrical response to a signal, had already taken place in his body. The full response had taken place before he could give a weak countersignal.

To understand such a process theoretically is not enough to free a person from the power of his conditioned reflex. It was not enough in the case of this young lawyer to help break a destructive habit at a decisive moment.

Even if it were theoretically possible to inhibit fully a destructive habit—a conditioned reflex—it would leave a person in a kind of vacuum of action or reaction. Our patient, in order to improve himself, had to act at the first link of the chain, then step-by-step recondition himself to new reflexes. Also, to avoid a vacuum, he had to find a substitute—that is, another response—and develop this into a new, useful pattern. Theoretically, a substitution would mean the creation of new and different mental and body responses to a given signal based on the freedom to examine and consider the realities of the situation. In actual practice, however, we have to struggle against the immense power of the well-established earlier habit responses. Nevertheless, in our growing-up process we prove that we can change them, and we are successful if we work continuously at it.

A patient of mine, a very bright young economist had changed her job and now felt almost paralyzed in her work by the stern authority of her new boss. She reacted to him with the same fear paralysis she felt when her cold, cynical father made a demand. Saying to herself "He is not my father" did not quite help her, but associating her new boss with kind old Uncle Henry helped her to substitute the threatening figure with a benevolent one, so that the new image caused in her, indeed, a new relaxed response and in due time a new confident habit.

Since the classic Greeks, from which so much of our culture is descended—and it may have been part of other cultures, too—the maxim "know thyself" has been treated as if it expressed the pinnacle of wisdom. At times, I have wondered if the truly wise who have said it have not done so tongue in cheek? The maxim sounds so plain and simple, yet the wisdom it contains advises one to undertake what is perhaps the most difficult curriculum of all.

Knowledge of anything exists for the most part of these two items: recognition and predictability. By the formula "A plus B equals C," for example, we recognize algebra. If we know the values of any two of these quantities we can know the value of the third. Because of our knowledge of principle we can predict the result.

Of the self, almost the only thing we can claim to know with confidence is our ability to change. We are always changing and, unless we deal with a neurotically very rigid marionette, we continue to change. This is growth. But even with the neurotically disturbed person there is no absolute standstill. There is either progression or retrogression regardless of how minute the change may be. It might be correct to paraphrase Descartes to read, "What I think, therefore, I am." We can, each one of us, be sure that five years from now what we think about many topics will be somewhat different from what we think today.

That is prediction. But recognition of the self is no easy matter. Who has not asked himself in puzzlement, "Why did I do that (or not do it?)" or, "What made me give this preposterous answer?" or, "How could I ever have

70

trusted this man, taken his advice, believed in his story, etc.?"

Because self-knowledge is difficult does not mean that it is beyond our reach. "Practice makes the master" is an old European proverb. Working on ourselves is continuously widening our horizon, and recognition of the four personality types is helpful in these attempts. Only giving up or not even making an attempt leads to failure.

No one is ever completely and exclusively any one of these four types. To be completely hostile would make us murderers; to be completely inhibited, suicides. The adjusted person is a combination of self-starting (aggressive), related (dependent), and self-controlled (inhibited) traits. Health and happiness is a matter of keeping the dynamic traits in balance. And overemphasis in any direction is a sign of unhappiness and illness.

When any such sign is discovered, the healthy individual knows that he must do something about his state of disturbed functioning. Frequent or chronic disturbances demand a change in the personality. This then is a matter of self-knowledge about where we stand and where we want to go. The acquiring of new attitudes is one process which brings about a change of personality; assimilation is another. Religious or political conversion is still another, and as a rule, forceful way of changing personalities, though, unless fear or external pressure is the cause, it is often not as dramatic and sudden as it may appear. For such conversions are usually preceded by long periods of discontent, or a growing readiness to change, or even a realization that a change has already unconsciously taken place. Such conversions become strong and permanent parts of the personality. Pavlov proved that when the conditioning of a dog is broken and is replaced by a new conditioning, the dog obstinately holds on to his new conditioning. We have ample evidence of similar experiences in man. Religious and political conversions often turn the converts into fanatics, unshakable in their new belief. Any attempt to change the acquired belief meets with obstinate resistance.

This is the theory behind the mysterious and intriguing process we call "brainwashing." It is the technique of changing a personality by breaking down conditioned reflexes through suasion or fear, thereby eliminating resistance and creating in its place a readiness to adopt a new line of

71

thought. Pavlov changed the personality type of his dogs by confusing them. He first accustomed them to certain signals, like the ringing of the bell when the dog was given his food, which by repetition produced a conditioned reflex. There were other signals which the dogs through experience learned to associate with pleasure or pain. When these signals were well-established and well-recognized by the dogs, Pavlov introduced variations. He would lengthen the time interval between signals, or he would change the intensity of the signals, or he would apply the signal to a different association. The dog, thus frustrated, became confused and, ultimately, torpid.

This is related experimentation again, to the process of protective inhibition. The brain cells, overexcited by their problem and their inability to solve it, simply stop working entirely before they might be seriously damaged by the pressure of confusion.

As Pavlov continued his studies of the effect of stress on reflexes, he established that reflexes can be conditioned by repetition of the same associated phenomena; that if the stress exceeds the endurance of the nervous system, a state of protective inhibition stops all nervous activity before the damage done can become perhaps irreparable; that this endurance varies from person to person (and dog to dog) according to the previously established personality type; and that the process of protective inhibition tends to erase effects of conditioning, leaving the mind blank, innocent, and susceptible to new impressions.

This is significant. As he expanded his studies, Pavlov established that dogs which suffered protective inhibition not only lost the conditioning which had previously been imposed on them, but also were more than previously susceptible to new conditioning. He conditioned his animals by using signals; classically a bell was rung each time a dog was given his food, or a light flashed, or some other signal was repeated so often that the signal and the action were inflexibly associated in the dog's mind. Dogs that survived the Neva flood had learned to recognize water in the kennel as a signal of danger.

Pavlov wrote: "The dogs suffered according to the type to which they belonged. The strong excitatory types were not disturbed, but the inhibitory lost all of their conditioned food reflexes, and some suffered to such a degree that we could not cure them." Terror made the inhibitory-type dogs lose their carefully conditioned pattern of behavior, as if their brain had been wiped clean. Pavlov repeated the experiment by letting a trickle of water run under the door of the cages. All the dogs and especially those who had lost their personality pattern became sensitive to the sight of water even after they had become normal.

He found that he could produce a protective inhibition in his dogs by any of four different methods: (1) by an increased intensity of the signal; (2) by a change in the time interval, frequency, or regularity of the signal; (3) by contradictory signals as when, in rapid succession, positive and negative signals were given and the dog became confused about which one to follow; and finally (4) by fatigue, by overworking the animal or exposing him to a variety of stresses, whether chemical, thermic, or mechanical, or by something physical or psychic calculated to cause fear, anger, despair, and similar prolonged emotional irritations.

Although they may seem to approach the problem of human personality from opposite directions, the teachings of Freud and Pavlov are not in opposition to one another. Lawrence F. Kubie, the noted American psychiatrist, stated that "the psychoanalytic technique of free association is actually the mirror image of the conditioned reflex itself."

The powerfully established first system of conditioned reflexes causes everyone throughout life to respond automatically and in a matter of microseconds to specific stimuli. The process of free association—which is the unselected verbalization by a patient of whatever comes to mind, and is used in psychoanalysis as a means of discovering the problem the patient has and to free him from his compulsions—reveals the sum of the stimuli which we later call habit, training, or education. Man responds to the fine nuances and to a vast array of stimuli as the conditioned animal would when it has been conditioned to a signal.

To show how very fine a distinction reflexes can make, a dog was given his food on the 124th beat of the metronome and would not salivate before that beat. In another experiment a dog was conditioned to take in food every thirteen minutes. That dog will react—that is, salivate—every thirteen minutes whether he receives food or not. There was one experiment in which a dog had been given morphine. As with many people, this drug produces nausea, followed by vomiting, then induces a profound sleep. After five or six days of injecting the dog with morphine, the dog would vomit and go to sleep before actually receiving the injection. All that was necessary for this dog was to see the doctor taking the hypodermic syringe out of the container.

Through the process of schooling, reading, observation, and thinking, each individual human being develops the pattern of his own specific personality, and through repetition the useful responses become conditioned reflexes. This complicated system enables us to live in an organized society, but also leads us into many conflicts: conflicts of religious beliefs and scientific principles; of prejudices and human rights; of blind spots, narrow-mindedness or the open-mindedness of the unbigoted intellect.

To some degree we are all prisoners of our conditioning. When this imprisonment produces conflicts injurious to health and happiness, then drastic measures to change the personality pattern become a need. In other words, when our personality, which is the sum of our conditioning, makes us unhappy and psychosomatically ill because of an overemphasis on hostility, dependency, or inhibition, we must try to change, either by ourselves or with help.

Since so many arch-orthodox people speak of the immutability of human nature, let us repeat that personality can be changed. Actually it is changing all the time, because we react to life, and life is not static, but dynamic. It may not always change for the better, because we tend to repeat what we do easily and successfully, and this repetition is performed so often without any opportunity for deliberation. Where personality creates trouble for us by causing us to magnify the obstacles to our happiness beyond their true worth and by permitting us to stay in a tangle of problems without cutting the Gordian Knot, the change must be made deliberately.

This is often done by providing artificial stimulation to the brain cells and inducing protective inhibition. For example, a troubled person may mesmerize himself with endless double-feature films or an overexposure to the sun on a beach or compulsive reading. Or it is done for us by nature when we experience symptoms of fatigue and, if unrelieved, a "nervous breakdown" which enforces rest and reappraisal.

Pavlov stated that he could produce conditions in his laboratory which resembled human schizophrenia and also that he had learned how to cure these conditions. The Leningrad flood had given him a first clue to the fact that fear could break a carefully conditioned pattern in animals, and could cause them to lose their resistance. An unscrupulous political regime was quick to recognize the far-reaching significance of this scientific principle in bringing about a forceful indoctrination and a new systematic change of beliefs, habits, and convictions.

The western world was astonished to read about the great public trials in the middle 1930s in Moscow, when the brilliant and ruthless Vishinsky, as the state's prosecutor, extracted signed confessions of treason from the accused, who not only admitted their guilt, but pleaded for their well-deserved punishments by death. This grim spectacle demonstrated the potential of brainwashing and how this principle could be used for evil, although it was intended for the ultimate benefit of man.

Because, presumably, brainwashing has been abused in certain cases, it is assumed that it is necessarily a wicked process, but this need not be the case. Pavlov's purposes were certainly quite the opposite. He hoped that his experiments would ultimately lead to the development of a better kind of human being, perhaps even the perfect man. He never dreamed that his findings could be used for dehumanizing purposes but rather hoped that they could help to produce a better and stronger type of individual, and thus benefit all mankind.

The principle of brainwashing, then, gives us a clue to how we can accomplish a change of behavior. We can correct signals by countersignals. By creating countersignals, we can learn to stem the automatic reactions of an involuntary conditioned reflex and substitute another, more desirable response.

Electric and insulin shock treatments needed for the more severe mentally ill are used in a similar way to eliminate recent frightening or traumatic experiences. Although the foremost authority on electric shock treatment in this country told me that no one actually knows what goes on in the brain, we may assume that it is perhaps Pavlov's process of protective inhibition and a change of chemical processes that bring about an easing of the psychic pain and a change of intolerable feeling processes.

Sometimes, as in certain brainwashing techniques, the

process of change can be swift, though brutal. Any real change of personality is painful because it is an uprooting process and because it has been made necessary by unhappiness and failure. We would do well to remember that our first conditioning was equally difficult and, perhaps, even more painful, although nature had helped us to forget the pain.

All our living and growing is a continuous conditioning process, one which, of course, diminishes in intensity as we go along. Most people have memories of humiliating and painful experiences either in their early life or their adolescence, so that we not infrequently hear someone say, in full sincerity, "I'm glad I'm not young anymore."

The inhibitory pattern of personality is especially tormenting, not only because of the repression of instinctual drives and the natural spontaneity, and the unbearable tensions, but also because it engenders constant doubts about oneself, whether one appears normal to others or even if one is in fact normal. The aggressive personality, encouraged by early successes, strikes out in an ever-widening variety of experiences, whereas the inhibited individual, feeling inadequate, awkward, and out of place, retreats into the same familiar restrictive pattern which promises safety and security but which is contrary to the freedom of self-expression and the pleasures of a dynamic life.

The inhibited personality may never succeed in becoming a really outgoing aggressive individual, but what is necessary is that, within the framework of the individual personality structure, he attains freedom from tensions and overcomes that strangling inner fear which holds him back from participating in social, civic, and other functions essential to a sense of belonging and well-being.

Some of the fear with regard to changing oneself is well justified, because changing a pattern is like changing a structure. It is the fear of the unknown, a fear of disillusionment, a fear of possibly suffering a crushing defeat. The fragile ego of many people simply cannot bear the thought of another failure. Evaluating their present unhappy situation, they know where their old shoe pinches them, and so they would rather carry on. They fear the possible collapse of the entire structure if a pillar is removed without replacing it with a stronger one. Every step of the way therefore we must consider all along the principle of "disengagement and substitution." For each habit we wish to change, we must have another healthier one ready, just as we would have a new and stronger beam ready to replace an old worn one we are about to eliminate.

"Disengagement" means a gentle, step-by-step removal of a habit of behavior rather than a violent uprooting of it. There are two schools of thought on breaking a powerful destructive habit: one is an abrupt discontinuation, the other a weaning away. A sensible decision will depend primarily on the personality type. When attempting to break a narcotic habit, for instance, or alcoholism, the gentler, weaning-away method will prove ineffective. The more successful approach, then, is an immediate and complete stop. But this method has a chance only if the person involved has, first of all, a genuine desire to change, and the determination and discipline to carry out such a decision. But then he must substitute a new, constructive activity for the old, destructive one. If he lacks the strength, he needs help.

In the process of classic psychoanalysis, patients were told to refrain from any important decision until they had gained enough insight. But, since such a process may take years, it means continuing a life of suspense. Many doctors are therefore changing their attitude. I, personally, am in the habit of telling my patients at the very beginning that each little step away from their old pattern weakens it, while each little step toward a new pattern strengthens that, and that a decision, even if it is not as yet an easy or a perfect one, is preferable to postponing it to a better, more opportune time.

Reconditioning is the changing of habits by relinquishing old attitudes for new ones. It is a process that requires constant repetition. The goal of the change must be kept before one's eyes all the time. This is necessary if we want to make the new habit as automatic as possible and if we wish to accomplish this in as quick a time as possible. While it is true that old habits have a magnetic power over us, it is also true that we can demagnetize and discard them. Only lack of knowledge and lack of confidence may make so many people abandon their efforts to overcome the power of inner resistance. They either give up their efforts too quickly or they approach their goal too haphazardly. In our attempts to adjust to life we all learn to control our impulses, and we all develop new responses in order to resolve the conflicts between the way we have been brought up—that is, conditioned—and the way we would like to be. It is when we cease to make further adjustments and cease to grow up that we become rigid and age prematurely. This is why we so often have a schism between the young and the old generation, the latter often complaining that they "don't understand these young people." This is unfortunate, for when we stop growing emotionally, when we stop integrating the simmering, heterogeneous forces of the inner self with the external realities of our lives and when we deny the very existence of conflicts between the two, we resist maturing, we resist the privilege of growing as human beings and of fully utilizing our potentials. We actually turn our backs on all hope of mastering our own destinies and of recovering our lost happiness.

I repeat, the course of life is change. All of us, except for the mentally disturbed, attempt to weed out obnoxious, destructive attitudes and struggle to replace them with more acceptable behavior.

All organic life is maintained by a continuous process of adaptation to new or changing outer conditions. This is a dynamic process, as is the child's efforts to emulate a parent or the stranger's ambition to assimilate to a new culture. The constant practice of habits have the power to turn superficial behavior into a conditioned reflex. Without our ability to adjust to a desirable reality we could not survive and without our ability to break undesirable destructive habits, any process of adjustment would be impossible. This means that in many little and undramatic ways throughout life we continuously make and break habits. But this also means that we can exchange an unhealthy and wasteful way of existence with a new and healthy pattern of productive living.

6.

What WOMEN Do to Men
—and MEN to Women

A WOMAN CAN DESTROY A MAN AND HE MAY NOT EVEN KNOW it. The patient who mumbled these words in a kind of introspective daze, hardly aware of their meaning, was speaking more to himself when he went on to say, "Now, I can understand why someone may feel like putting a bullet right into his head and ending it all. When you can't sink lower than the belly of a snake, all you want is peace . . ."

His eyes, which had the look of a wounded animal, changed quickly to an expression of defiance when he pulled himself together to answer the question of why a man would allow a woman the power to destroy him.

"In my case it was all my fault," he said. "I could not give her what she wanted. When I leave my place of work, I am six feet tall; when I enter my home, I shrink to four. Now it is the same at work. I am just a failure."

In a merciless, masochistic mood of self-condemnation, he went on to defend his wife's infidelities and her contemptuous little digs at him. He had forgotten that he had feebly resisted being forced into marriage by her having become pregnant, and he was not aware that under the mask of charm was an unhappy woman who was at war with all men because she wanted to be a man herself.

This patient had a long way to go before he could recognize why he put women on a pedestal, then readily submitted to their power, and how he could go about regaining his lost self-confidence and develop the stature of a secure male.

Another man, also struggling against a growing feeling of inadequacy, took another line of defense to bolster his weakened position. He blamed his wife, not himself, for all his troubles. All his failures and frustrations, he said, were due to her lack of understanding of him, and her inability to help him and to give of herself.

This man, like the first one we have just briefly described, was also in his mid-thirties. However, he was at first reluctant to talk about his unhappiness and thought that his feelings of exhaustion were due to some physical causes which doctors could not explain. He tired easily; he found it more and more difficult to get up in the morning and to concentrate once he was up, and he feared for his future. What baffled him most was that when he was on vacation or fishing, he felt strong and energetic, so much so that he believed himself to be capable of doing almost anything. But lately he had become more and more irritated and depressed. Both at home and at work he felt that his disappointments were out of proportion to the satisfactions he had a right to expect. About his domestic life he admitted wishing that his wife would give up her job to take care of the children instead of turning them over to a governess. Under questioning, it developed that his wife was not just holding a job, but followed a creative career in the field of fashion, and that her income actually surpassed his. Without her contribution they could not afford to live the way they did.

His own job was that of copy editor for a large advertising concern. In it he was both a big wheel to the copywriters and a small cog to the executives. Whatever satisfaction he got out of being the editor was destroyed by his immediate superior, "a high-powered, cynical, mannish kind of a 'dame.' She causes a lot of tensions; she is overcritical. I don't mind her being overcritical," he said, "because I can stand criticism. I've had it all my life. But when I do give her what she wants, she has a way of punching holes in it and getting cynical about it. To her, a good piece of work is a brilliant kind of flytrap sales program. It makes me wonder if I'm a copy editor or a fakir selling a miraculous snake oil."

Then—let's call him Ralph—he talked at great length about his physical symptoms. He elaborated on his frequent states of fatigue, which forced him to go to bed on his return from the day's work at his office. This was a conversion—that is, a physical manifestation of his repressed sexual wishes, his anger against his wife's frigidity, and a bit of regression against the unkindness of his external world, the boss, the office, and, lately, his home. His wife served him dinner on a tray. He considered this natural, since he was so tired. He had no conscious awareness of his aloofness. He did not know that his withdrawal from the family table was a symptom of rejection of his wife and children, and an act of unconscious hostility against them because of the responsibility they burdened him with. He felt justified to be resentful.

Ralph's feelings of exhaustion had no physical basis. Other people work the same hours; so did his wife who, when she came home, prepared dinner, brought his tray to him in the bedroom where he watched television. Then she fed the children and put them to bed.

Ralph was exhausted not because of his work as such, but because of the resentment he carried against his boss, and the fear he had that his feelings would be discovered and he could then be fired. Instead of admitting this to himself, he rationalized that it was the responsibility of his job that exhausted him and also that the work was beneath his dignity. He was not aware of his resentment of his wife and children, for instead of sharing a meal and all the small daily experiences together, he rationalized his hostility by complaining that the children were too lively and too noisy— which they probably were—for his sensitive nerves, which were so "tender" because of what happened inside him. The fact is, Ralph was actually competing with his children for the attention and pampering a child needs but an adult should have outgrown, and since he felt he could not be the center of attention, he preferred to create for himself a state of physical isolation. He justified his attitude by saying that his wife and even his young children treated him with no respect or appreciation. Their respective attitudes fed upon each other, the way an argument grows from simple disagreement past the point of reconcilement and into open bitter dispute.

The area in which Ralph's conflict had become acute, but which at the same time he tried most to deny, was the sexual. Instead of facing himself as the affectionally estranged, resentful, and weak man he was, he blamed his wife for all the inadequacies that existed in their mutual life. Such projection is a defense mechanism; it attributes to a matter one's own unacceptable emotions, and not only pursues them as real in the other, but reacts to them as if

81

they were objective realities. The man who believes "the whole world is against me" is actually working against the rest of the world instead of trying to find some mutually acceptable working arrangement. Or when he says, "No one likes me," he means, without himself realizing it, that he likes no one. When a patient of mine once remarked, "My problem is that my boss does not cooperate," he really meant that he himself resisted cooperation. But where such projection so often becomes insidious and dangerous is within the family. When a husband or wife accuses the other of "pushing" to a point of collapse, the complainant may be pushing himself, because of some obscure guilt or resentment or fear, and then blames the other.

When Ralph blamed his wife for being cold, it was really he who was aloof and cold and who isolated himself, then felt cut off, unloved, and insignificant. These feelings made him angry and encouraged him to indulge in his fantasy of considering himself exceptional.

Let us take another example. An attractive, slim, blonde, blue-eyed woman of thirty turned in despair to her gynecologist because she felt she could not go on with her life. This doctor in turn referred his patient to me. Ever since her first baby girl was born, four years before, the relationship between herself and her husband had deteriorated. She described him as a brilliant engineer who was actually jealous of his child, although he at the same time adored her.

The husband's interest toward his wife had cooled considerably, and she felt that she herself had lost her sexual interest in him. For the past year she had been aware that her husband was carrying on an intimate relationship with another woman, the wife of a mutual friend, whom she had thought of as her best friend. The past half year or so she had become depressed because she believed that she loved her husband and her child, but felt that a wall had grown up between them and herself which she found impossible to break down. Because she had withdrawn from her husband, she felt that the estrangement was somehow her fault. She had considered returning to her native Canada, but felt ashamed to allow her family to see her coming home as a failure. She told her husband that perhaps they should see a doctor or a psychiatrist to find out why they had drifted apart and whether a reconciliation could not be effected. In her unhappiness, she even thought that perhaps a second child might help, a suggestion which her husband brusquely brushed aside as being out of the question because it would just be an added financial responsibility which, she should know, they could not afford. She did not believe this to be the true reason and took his rejection as a personal rebuff. She became convinced that he did not really care at all about her, their home, or their family life.

In her mind, she linked this latest rejection to his other earlier negative attitudes toward her as when, with a group of friends, he neglected paying attention to her, or when he found excuses for not coming home at night far more frequently than she thought justified, or when he was late for dinner because he had been having a drink with some business associates, or when on vacation he would leave her and the baby alone in their rented cottage while he went off on fishing trips with some of his friends.

In her unhappiness she felt as if gripped by an unshakable fatigue, which made it difficult to get out of bed in the morning, and to take care of the child and the home. Everything she had enjoyed—cooking, shopping, reading, or receiving guests—was an effort. She would burst into tears at the slightest provocation, and feel her heart pounding and her body trembling. She slept badly, was plagued by nightmares, and had lost her appetite.

Encouraged to examine her feelings, she became aware of the tremendous hostility she was harboring, a feeling in herself which was doing her great harm, regardless of whether her husband's attitudes were right or wrong, justified or not.

Here we see the two ever-moving forces of life, excitation and inhibition, perilously clashing with one another. While under normal conditions these two forces function in a dynamic state of balance, the power of excitation in our patient began to break through her controlling inhibition.

She was hospitalized to remove her from the irritating environment and oppressive duties, and to provide the rest which would allow her partially paralyzed brain cells to recover.

She recovered quickly. After a few days she began to feel stronger, and in a little over a week she wanted to go home. But a new perspective seemed to have changed the picture. She now insisted that she despised her husband and had no love left for him. He in turn, having been brought up by an overindulgent mother, became frightened by her changed attitude. He insisted that he loved his wife. He felt sorry about his irresponsibility, and insisted that more than anything else in the world he wanted to maintain his home and his marriage.

The wife was ready to accept psychotherapeutic treatment. She wanted to understand the reasons for her withdrawal, her change of attitude, as well as the true nature of her churning hostilities. She needed to learn what to do with these turbulent feelings and why she would provoke her husband at a time when he needed reassurance. Had she not, by her passivity and withdrawal, driven him into the arms of another woman? The understanding of the milieu and the behavior of the people during her formative years made her realize how her sense of inadequacy had come about. She learned to relate some of her fears and her need to withdraw to specific attitudes or demands of people. With this clarity she slowly learned to adopt a more assertive behavior and practiced with determination how to overcome her crippling feelings of self-defeat and depression, and how to assert herself more as an adult woman.

One strange phenomenon in this process was the radical change in her opinion of her husband. Once the fear paralysis had left her, she could see him with a frightening objectivity as the immature, weak and irresponsible man he was. As her fear faded, so did her respect for him. Now she wanted another, stronger man who could take care of her and provide her with the security she so ardently longed for.

Her growing self-assurance confused her husband; more so because they did not talk about their problem. His behavior changed from indifference, to inquiry, to anxiety. He became more and more anxious. He kept wondering what had happened and tried to discourage his wife from having further treatments. She remained adamant about this and he now had no choice other than to learn how to cope with the changed home situation, his self-assured wife, and the new problems which had arisen.

The husband made the disquieting discovery that he had deluded himself into believing that he could live an "independent" life when in fact to function effectively he needed the support of a home, a family, and a protective, more aggressive woman. A great deal of goodwill was necessary to remove the wall that the woman, more so than the man. felt had developed between them and to build a new basis for a more meaningful relationship. The one hopeful sign was that both people were aware of their mutual need. Both feared to be alone and because of this showed willingness to work toward an understanding of one another.

A third example of the unhappy husband-wife theme is a woman who looked younger than her forty-seven years. She was stylishly dressed, although she said that she and her husband were living in rather modest circumstances. He was an automobile salesman who had come to this appointment with his wife because she was afraid to travel alone. He was a heavy-set man, biting rigidly on a dead cigar while his wife told her story.

"I don't know where to begin," she said. "And, worse, I don't know anymore what is important and what is unimportant." Prior to her first visit she had seen a number of physicians. All her life she had had migraine headaches; injections with gynergen, an alkaloid, used to help this condition but then she had developed a revulsion to injections. Two years earlier she had been to the New York Medical Center for treatment of her thyroid deficiency. There was a short-lived improvement, then she lapsed back into a state of exhaustion. Another doctor had given her marsalid tablets—subsequently withdrawn from the market because of their dangerous side effects. This had a miraculous effect for three months, but then led to a state of weakness and shakiness. The family physician thought she had Asiatic flu, but another doctor expressed his suspicion that the marsalid had poisoned her. She had taken tranquilizers, which caused dryness and other distressing symptoms.

At the present time, the patient was so feeble that she was tottering on her feet; she didn't dare go out and felt unable to take care of the household. She had been married twenty-four years and had three children who were all in college. For the past ten years, the atmosphere at home had become unbearable, she said. She had recognized her husband's heavy dependency on her and the increasing demands he made on her. He said that after a long day's work he was tired, that he enjoyed staying home reading his papers or watching his favorite programs on television. She had given up almost all her friends and interests because of his complaints that she neglected him.

That patient had a variety of physical symptoms, such as a very low blood pressure, a very high cholesterol content in her blood, and a low thyroid function, and wondered whether they were the cause or result of her disturbed emotional state.

Her main problem, she said, was her state of utter frustration in living with a man who over the years had more and more restricted every attempt she made to gain some independence. For the sake of peace and the children, she suppressed her growing resentment. She had long ago lost respect for her husband, but she did not know that her resentment had grown into hate. Hate was a terrifying and unacceptable term to her, and, yet, talking about their home life made her realize that both of them carried on a poorly concealed, ruthless, and continuous guerilla warfare.

Areas of communication and mutual interest had long since been lost, or perhaps had never even had a chance to develop. Their distorted concept of love was to render each other ineffective because of each one's insecurity and other immature needs.

When the patient returned, she said that the last visit had a delayed reaction as if she had been hit by both barrels. This was her dramatic way of stressing her realization of the truth of the relationship with her husband. She faced up to the fact that a mere treatment of physical symptoms alone would not bring her the peace and happiness she desired, but would, besides wasting money, end in a new disappointment. So stirred up did she feel as a result of the disturbing afterthoughts that she could not sleep for several nights. For the first time in her life she dared to admit openly that she hated someone. This awareness had shaken the beliefs she had had about herself. After days of a "terrific upheaval" she said that she had felt elated and for two days was actually free from headaches.

The first change to a more optimistic outlook came when she admitted her hostility openly. She realized that her disturbing physical symptoms were caused not simply by her loss of respect for her husband, but by the awareness that he was not taking care of her, that she could not trust his judgment, that she felt betrayed and, yet, was trapped in this relationship. She came to realize that her initial anger toward me had been caused by her becoming aware of a truth and her conflict, with all its disturbing complications, which she had heretofore denied. Her dilemma caused her intense anxiety. She knew she could not change the man. She feared for the future. She was fearful of leaving him and rejected the idea, yet she could not accept the idea of continuing to live with a man who was always changing jobs, who always had some great new project which never materialized.

This man and the woman were actually living for the purpose of irritating each other. Unable to create anything that could satisfy their neurotic wants, they needed one another as targets on which to release their restless, hostile drives, and into these battles went the major part of their energy. They needed one another for negative reasons. The power to hurt one another confirmed the fact of their wasteful existence. She gave an example of a scene at home:

"I used to love to cook. I just loved to prepare a meal with thought and at leisure, but one day I gave up. It seemed that each time I was ready to serve the dinner my husband always had to go to the bathroom. What a man can do there for a full hour, I don't know. I used to wait. The food got cold and the pleasure was gone. He left me perturbed, and frustrated."

There was no pleasure in this marriage for her husband either. He too felt disappointed. He was not aware of his constant neurotic need for self-assertion, by rebelling against his wife similar to the way his father had rebelled against his mother. And he did not know that behaving the way he did, meant acting contrary to his own best interests. This was his conditioning. Emotionally, these two grown people were children who, because they could not get what they wanted for themselves, punished their respective parent substitute by thrusting their dissatisfactions on to their spouse in order to ameliorate their own neurotic suffering.

The responsibilities of adult life—marriage, children, economic necessities—would not allow this woman to leave her husband even though in many ways she was as childish as he was. Her rejection of divorce was rationalized as a consideration for her children but was actually caused by her fear of loneliness and by her doubt that she could find another man at her age.

The husband was an even more dependent person. He needed his wife both to take care of him and to torment her. Besides the sadistic pleasure this gave him, it permitted him a feeling of release of aggression and to prove his power. His wife played the perfect masochist counterpart to his sadism, although she was not conscious of the fact that with her distorted sense of martydom she enjoyed suffering. She therefore bluntly rejected the idea that anyone would like to be hurt.

By doing nothing about her husband's neurotic behavior this woman was becoming increasingly more hopeless while at the same time she actually supported his neurosis.

What was she to do, she demanded to know? Why not serve dinner at the set time and, when her husband did not appear, eat and leave the house? Such an active step would have required a corresponding action on his part: either he ate the rest of the cold food later on alone or he had to give up his punitive, slipping away into the bathroom. Besides a lessening of provocation, such action would also prevent the use of a single harsh word or threat of violence, and a similar response in the other. It could perhaps even lead to a first step toward one another on the part of two people who could not part because they had a sick need for one another.

One reason why a husband may attack his wife, or a wife may turn against her husband is that a husband or wife may feel driven by a compulsive need to hurt the parent of the opposite sex in the spouse. A man may keep on punishing his mother image in his wife for all the rejection he has suffered, and a woman may punish her husband for all the disappointments she has experienced because her father had let her down.

Another insidious cause for continuous clashing is the unconscious competitiveness between the sexes. It exists when a woman feels compelled to live out her unconscious masculine identification, and when a man tries to behave according to his feminine conditioning. As a rule, there is little easing of tension because of the inability of the two people to communicate with each other. After all, their automatic reaction to set signals of provocation makes them feel that their response is natural. They cannot see the psychodynamic interplay. And so only too often one person's neurotic behavior only increases the feelings of unfairness, hurt and unhappiness in the other.

I remember an incident which took place when I had

been in practice only a few years. I asked a man with silvery white hair why he did not put a stop to his wife's extravagant and irresponsible behavior which so greatly upset him. After a thoughtful pause he answered sadly and resignedly: "Perhaps you are too young to understand. But believe me, I have tried everything. I worshipped her and so I tried kindness. Later on, I used threats, and finally, bribes. Yet nothing would change her behavior. She could not be reached. I loved her and could never think of leaving her, but perhaps it would have been better for both of us. Perhaps she was too frightened of men, and perhaps I had been too impatient or too inexperienced with her. No matter. I could never live up to the idol of a man she had formed in her fantasy." Actually in this case, the man had grown up without a mother; she died when he was a boy. He had never seen a good man-woman relationship. She on the other hand had been pushed into the marriage by an ambitious mother because of the material success the man had made. Not being in love with him she kept on opposing him.

Oppositional behavior is a much more serious emotional problem than rebellious conduct. Primarily, the rebel resists conventional or authoritative attitudes in order to assert himself and to protect his self-respect, even if this is done in an immature manner. Oppositional behavior goes far beyond such needs. It is always motivated by a need to contradict anyone, even to the point of expressing an opinion that may be in opposition to his own belief. Such a person feels compelled to say black, although he knows the color is really white.

Pavlov gave an explanation for such abnormal behavior. He called a response "paradoxical" in which the brain tends to react more to weak stimuli than to strong stimuli. He termed behavior "ultra-paradoxical" when conditioned positive responses become negative or when negative responses become positive.

Paradoxical behavior is found in a weak inhibitory type. For example, with dogs—an animal would go away when called and when told to go away, would come. When food is presented to him he would not take it but when the food is taken away he would search for it.

Paradoxical or oppositional behavior is at the root of many miserable and perplexing human relationships. Many men have been court-martialed and even executed for cowardice or mutinous behavior. Yet, these men could not help but react in such opposite ways because of their emotional illnesses. It is understandable how much unhappiness an oppositional behavior can cause in a marriage, as in the case of the man and his extravagant wife. It makes impossible the development of any human communication and any really meaningful relationship.

When a woman lashes out to hurt a man and a man lashes out to hurt a woman, it is for emotional and—most of the time—sexual reasons, not for those rationalized explanations so frequently offered as a reason. Freud has given us a most significant clue to the psychodynamics at work in such a situation.

A girl, according to psychoanalytic studies, is said to experience an Oedipus complex similar to the experience so called. Some analysts have used the term "Electra complex," but the majority seem to prefer the term "negative Oedipus complex" for describing the most significant phase in the psycho-sexual development of a girl.

When people say that they feel attracted to one another it is often for reasons of sexual desire, which many confuse with "love." Generally, the girl who has had a domineering mother grows up to dominate her husband in a manner similar to that in which mother dominated father. And the boy who experienced a domineering mother is most likely to seek out a girl who in personality is like mother.

Some thousand people, *The New York Times* reported (June 7, 1963), watched in disbelief as a masked junior keeper of the Bronx Zoo was adopted as a "mother" by three goslings who had seen nothing but their incubation box. After pecking out of their eggs, they followed the first large creature they saw—the junior keeper—and, as he walked, they paddled after him. When he trotted, they trotted; when he ran, they ran. This is one of the curiosities of nature.

We, as people do the same by conditioning, but, of course, we are conditioned to an infinitesimally more complex and detailed degree brought about by the natural closeness of living together. When a woman marries a man and believes his facade of strength to be real, she may feel disillusioned when she later finds out that he is emotionally dependent on her. She then may want to get away from him, only to find out that she is trapped by outer obstacles such as marriage, children, economic considerations, etc. Sometimes such a woman looks for the "ideal" man either in an extramarital affair or in a new husband. But, since nothing in her psychological make-up has changed, she often chooses the same type of personality in a different framework and repeats her old pattern in a second or third marriage. What such a woman may fail to know is that her attraction to the seemingly strong man had been due to her unconscious awareness that he is not really strong, but weak, or passive or dependent, and can be conquered. Whenever this type of woman meets a so-called "strong"— that is masculine, self-assured man—she is afraid, runs from the scene, and says, "I don't like him; he probably is a brute."

The similar setting in reverse exists for the man who seeks out a mother figure who can protect him. But, because he puts her on a pedestal, he then dreams of a more seductive type of woman whom he can conquer in order to prove his masculinity and gratify his sexual needs.

The cases presented here are people who have been in conflict with their partner of the opposite sex because of their confusion in accepting the role nature gave them as man or woman and of the conflict within themselves with regard to sex. There are of course, endless variations on the theme.

Many women resist sex not only because they consider it "dirty" and "sinful," but because they consider it "an act of submission" and resent "being used," a term most frequently used by women who are frigid.

Similarly, men have trouble with sex because of their unconscious fear of castration, or domination or ridicule by women, or because of their own passivity, which makes them extremely shy with women whom they fear they might hurt or be unworthy of. Others despise women because they consider them to be exploiting, devouring, and "seductive bitches," who do not give of themselves, but have a need to get, and are not really interested in making the sexual act a gratifying experience.

We term the people we have described "neurotic," but in no case were they extreme in their conduct. Whatever the outward expression of their belligerence or need to hurt one another, underneath, all these unhappy people were searching for an acceptable way of coexisting just as much as any of the rest of humanity. In cases where we do find extreme behavior, we can detect outright sadism in women against men and in men against women, all driven by an inner force they so often don't understand. Perhaps the two extreme types of sexual antagonists may explain some of the existing dynamics. They are known to us by the terms "call girl" and "Don Juan."

The call girl is a prostitute who does not openly solicit men on the street or operate in a house of prostitution. But while there may be among call girls women who enjoy sex or who, like the nymphomaniac, are in a continuous state of sexual excitation without real gratification, the emotional motivation for the call girl's way of life is an unconscious need to seek vengeance for having been born a girl, that is, not to possess a penis. Psychoanalytically, the girl's Oedipal phase is explained as a result of her childhood disappointment by her father who rejected her and leaves her with a drive to avenge herself upon every man. Girls who had a good loving and trusting relationship with their fathers grow up to be healthy women.

To be able to go from man to man, a woman must be frigid, or as in the case of the nymphomaniac, neurotically unsatisfied. This is part of a need to remain emotionally uninvolved or of being unable to build a relationship with a man, and to give her body only but not her inner self. Thus, the prostitute, often respectably married, strives to reduce the importance of that part of her body which she so deeply disrespects, as if she wanted to punish it. Also, through this most despised act of "love," if you can call it that, she intends to humiliate the male, who is accepted not for himself, but for the money he must pay to possess her for a short period of time. Her act and attitude satisfy her morbid need because this type of sex has been termed to be symbolically a mass castration of all men.

In a medical practice it is not too rare to meet male patients who confess that they have difficulty in having satisfactory sexual relations with their wives but have no problems with a prostitute, and who often live out their sexual needs in such a way. This is particularly true in cases in which the man had a strong neurotic attachment to his mother, and has married a mother image or turned his wife into a mother symbol. The reason why these men, in such relationships, feel uninhibited is that the prostitute is a type

92

of woman for whom they need not feel any respect or tenderness, who does not require courting, and who, psychologically, is not in any competition with them; therefore, they don't have to prove themselves worthy or effective. The upbringing of these men has generally stressed a forbidding attitude towards sex, mostly on the part of the mother, who regarded sex as a "lewd," "base," and a "beastly" function. One finds that men who grow up in such an environment often develop an image of two types of women: mothers and whores.

A girl in her mid-twenties showed a pattern of either suffering from severe asthma attacks and depressions or temporarily going into prostitution. Either of these conditions was provoked by a conflict with her mother. The girl shared with her mother a hostility toward men. Because of the coldness and the complete rejection she experienced from her father, she readily confessed that she hated men. She lived alone, but she had to be on good behavior and live according to the strict standards of her socially ambitious mother because she was financially dependent on her mother.

When pressures of the conflicts between mother and daughter became too intense, the mother would threaten the girl by withholding money. Then the girl would indulge in very active prostitution to punish or embarrass the mother and to prove to the mother that she did not need her money. The mother could not be hurt more deeply than to have even a suspicion of what her daughter might be doing, but the girl made sure that her mother had not a suspicion, but a certainty. Helpless, they had to find a way of reconciliation, which could only be the restoration of the girl's allowance. This generally lasted for a few months ending with a repetition of the earlier pattern.

The male counterpart of the call girl is the Don Juan. The fascinating symbol of the great lover and seducer is psychologically a male who feels insecure and therefore has a need to prove himself over and over as a well-functioning man. Or he has a deep-seated contempt for women, and his constant drive to conquer another woman, then leave her, is motivated by the hostility and disrespect he has for all women. His unconscious drive is to avenge himself for the disappointment he experienced from the first woman he ever knew—his mother.

Of all the Gordian Knots we tie for ourselves in this world the most numerous, complicated, endless, baffling, provoking, and fascinating is the marriage knot. Even to those who elude it, the spinsters and bachelors, it remains a subject of paramount interest. The marriage knot of our parents is of lifelong importance to us for its influence not only on our heredity, but also on the evironmental factors and the example they, as people, have given us. The marriage knot our friends tie for themselves is important to us. The knot we tie for ourselves is most important of all. Even when this knot is severed by divorce, as Alexander cut the Gordian Knot by a stroke of his sword, it remains part of our lives.

"I hate him because I love him! Can't you understand that?" said the character in a play. As I sat there in the audience, my first thought was, "No I can't. I find it hard to understand." The play was not a very good one. But I thought I knew what the author had perhaps meant to say—that there exists a mixture of both love and hate, called ambivalence, which is directed at some person at the same time and which we all learn when we grow up. The inability of the child to hate fully because he is too dependent on those he hates, and the difficulty to love fully because of the many hurts and rejections he experiences from those he loves leads to a fusion of both into one double feeling of loving a little less and hating a little less—hence ambivalence.

Generally, when we speak of love and hate we think of opposing twin peaks of emotion. In the valley between them lies indifference. We can be ambivalent, but we cannot love someone and at the same time be indifferent to them, or hate and be indifferent. Genuine love or hate implies an absence of indifference. We are involved and we feel a need to move toward someone or against someone, except for the frightened or the angry, who move away from those they love or hate.

This is what I remind myself of in the many cases of trouble between the sexes that are called to my attention. It sometimes seems as though I were more a marriage counselor than a doctor of medicine. But when people have problems it does no good to tell them to talk things over calmly, to make a compromise or to separate. There is in these cases always a problem that is part of the personality. This problem or conflict must be understood so that a decision can be made and energy can be released, not to fight one another, but in the positive, to reach a mutually acceptable goal and a good life; in the negative, to leave one another so that each has a chance to mature.

7.

ESCAPES

WHEN WE SPEAK OF "ESCAPE" WE GENERALLY EQUATE THE term, at least in a psychological sense, with an evasion of responsibility or of making a decision because of an acute need to seek mental relief. We escape danger, boredom, and responsibility in order to remain well. Or we think in terms of taking to flight, like getting away, or even death. When we use the term "escape" we must be more specific and ask ourselves what we are escaping from and where are we going?

Here again we can apply Claude Bernard's principle of the symptom of adaptation often turning into a disease of adaptation. A cigarette, a drink, a drug, a holiday may under certain circumstances bring us immense relief and can indeed greatly diminish a momentary state of stress which would otherwise harm us. This is protective. But a ceaseless continuation of such reliefs as chain smoking, drinking beyond the immediate feeling of relief, using drugs to keep oneself in a twilight state, loafing through a never-ending stretch of holidays under the disguise of exploring life but actually designed to avoid the assumption of one's daily responsibilities—all these habits and activities which started out to be protective then become a disease of adaptation. The same applies to food, sex, gambling, merry-making, and isolation.

While our yearly vacation or fishing trip, or even a movie or a cocktail party may be, in a strict sense, an escape, and a healthy one, we shall apply the term "escape" here when it is used as a palliative for unhappiness and when the so-called cure turns into a curse.

Man's harmful habits are an expression of his self-destructive drive. If we examine our common escapes we find that they are substitutes for existing needs, mostly neurotic in nature. We also find that they can be related to the four types of personality. The need for escape relates to one or the other of the two great forces of life, stimulation and relaxation, or in physiological terms, excitation and inhibition. In the last analysis, the first is an expression of life, the other an indication of moving in the direction of death.

When we run into a serious problem, an indecision, a block that wears us out, we may feel the need for a booster or an escape—that is, for an extra piece of candy, an extra drink, or a celebration of some sort—and these palliatives become stimulants if we wish to overcome the problem. We all are in need of some temporary relief. On the other hand, when we feel exhausted by an inner struggle and when we fear that we might break under the strain, we may tend to overdo or go in the opposite direction. We may be using perhaps the same means to help the natural process of inhibition, which is to secure the effective survival of our brain cells and in order to relax, to calm down, to get away from a disturbing situation we may seek oblivion. We want to go to sleep. We may drink or take pills to accomplish this. We want to do these things to get over a desperate crisis. We may not care whether we live or die. Actually we want to live, yet, for a small stretch of time we want to be "dead" to the world.

In regard to escape, the aggressive type of personality will react differently than the passive or withdrawn type. The first type will seek alleviation with the intent of taking up the battle again. The latter type, because of his difficulty or inability to make a decision, is more prone to seek escape along the ways of forgetfulness and of getting away from it altogether.

Most of the time escapes are chosen for emotional rather than physical reasons. Or escapes are motivated by specific needs. The habit of smoking is a conventional means of escape. It is said to be a relief from tension but it is useful up to a point only and in the light of new research it is potentially dangerous and self-destructive. When I was a medical student I learned that nicotine could cause unhealthy changes in the arterial system, and I wondered why people, having this knowledge, continued to smoke. What filled me with greater wonder was that the professor

97

who taught these facts was himself a smoker. This seemed to me just as one of the many baffling examples in life of "Do as I say, but not as I do."

Then I learned that it is "sophisticated" to smoke; that smoking is useful as a device to win time. As one of my patients, a famous actor, said, "It gives my restless hands something to do." When he stopped smoking, he grew a moustache, and his habit of twirling it became the characteristic by which he was known.

In the meantime, we have gained evidence that cigarettes are a contributory, if not the main cause, of lung cancer and of heart diseases. I personally believe that other factors, such as the type of personality and a state of depression, of futility or hopelessness must be considered as well and help to prepare the ground for the allergic or chemical or perhaps viral causes that produce this or an allied disease. It is my own experience that the passive-dependent and withdrawn personality types seem to be more prone to cancer than the aggressive or adjusted personalities, but, on the other hand, the former two types are more likely to seek escape in smoking as they are in overeating, drinking too much or nibbling candy.

In a paper of mine published in 1960 in both *Transactions of the New York Academy of Sciences*, and *Psychosomatics*, the official publication of the Academy of Psychosomatic Medicine, I referred briefly to a discussion I had with Professor V. Fedorov at the Pavlov Institute after he had stated that rabbits, classified as "inhibitory animals," showed a more rapid development of malignant growths than did "excitable, inert animals." I asked the Russian professor if in his observation "depressed or hopeless" animals were more prone to cancer or if they showed a greater progress of the disease, whereupon with a slight smile and an emphatic nod of his head, he said "tak, tak . . ."—that is, "yes, yes."

When people smoke, they say that they do so for pleasure. Patients who have been advised to quit smoking often claim that they have tried to stop but have always fallen back into the grip of their addiction. Some patients simply say that they can't stop because they just like to smoke. Yet, when so advised, they can give up other things, like certain types of food, or other habits. What then is the deeper reason for so many people's insatiable hunger for cigarettes in view of and in spite of the grave warnings that they may be inviting their own destruction?

Psychoanalysts say that smoking is a sublimation of a vibrant sexual need and a symbol for the gratification which the infant experiences when he puts his mother's nipple in his mouth. It is associated with pleasure, food, comfort, and security. It was Freud's genius which discovered that sexuality begins the day the child is born and, although it does undergo various changes, never ends until he dies.

The first, "oral" stage of sexuality is said to last from birth through the twelfth month or so. It is expressed by the child's sucking his thumb after a meal, thus prolonging the pleasure (perhaps like a cigarette or a cigar after dinner). Later on, it may be that the thumb-sucking is continuous, like chain smoking. In some cases we know that the sucking lasts until the kindergarten age or even later.

Orality includes both of the human's most basic feelings, those of love and hate or, as the analyst terms them, erotic and sadistic motivations. In the baby, the first of these is expressed by the pleasurable sucking and the other by the attempts, when displeased, to bite with his still weak and toothless mouth. These two emotions continue throughout life in a sublimated or disguised form: in kissing and cursing; in singing or in making biting speeches; in eating, drinking, and chewing; or in angrily biting one's nails or grinding one's teeth.

Over the years I have come to relate the smoking habit in my patients to their strong emotional needs. The smoking habit may be either a substitute for sexual cravings or a need for pleasure, or for comfort. It may be a "bracer" to meet some unwelcome but unavoidable unpleasantness. Time and again I have observed a patient speak calmly about various relevant matters until the discussion took a turn toward either his father or mother, to whom the patient inevitably had strong emotional attachments, at which point there is a hasty fumbling and out comes the cigarette, which must be hurriedly lit, especially when the relationship with a parent had been a negative one.

There are patients who get in such a state of anxiety when they talk about their emotional lives during their consultation that they actually become chain smokers, and I must empty a full ashtray before my next patient enters the office. With one patient I counted two cigarette butts under ordinary conditions but always five butts when we talked about her mother.

The oral character of smoking becomes quite evident

when a person gives up his cigarettes and then begins quickly to put on weight. As a young doctor, I had the naive belief that this gain in weight was due to the elimination of the poison in the cigarettes which had killed the appetite. Today I believe that there exists a lesser need for excess food if the oral sexual need is gratified by cigarettes. It is only when we realize that cigarettes have an important and significant effect in answering many stirring emotions which the individual feels compelled to control that we can understand the obstinancy with which people cling to this habit, even when they are warned that it may cost them their lives.

A case which illustrated such addiction was a woman who seemed to have everything to live for, but who inwardly felt haunted, deprived, and discouraged, and so was making her way along a lonely road toward self-destruction. Let us call her Harriet. She was attractive. married, and had two good-looking, intelligent sons. Harriet had a career. Years ago, she had become known all over the country as a result of the delightful comedy roles she played in a number of successful plays on Broadway and on the road.

She told me that she was happy and had every reason to be so. Her second marriage, she said, was a successful one, and she referred to her husband proudly as a "man's man." The older of her two boys was considered an outstanding student, and the younger excelled in sports. Over and beyond her professional duties, she was much sought after as an organizer of charitable functions. She was capable of displaying a dynamic enthusiasm which could turn a lagging charity drive into a successful affair.

The reason for her visit to my office, she was quick to explain, was really very trivial. Indeed, had not a friend been so foolishly worried and insistent, she would not have come at all. To please her friend she did come, but all she really needed, if I could give it to her, was some professional advice on how to stop smoking. She insisted that she wanted a "magic formula" rather than a detailed exploration of what might be troubling her. She hardly concealed her chagrin at having to ask for help in the first place. She resented being in a position of speaking about her own personal feelings. She was not unlike many other outwardly strong personalities who resent being made conscious of a hopeless position and turn their resentment against their helper.

I asked her to tell me why she wanted to stop smoking, and what her difficulty was in quitting. She had developed a pain in her legs, she said, which at times was so intense that it forced her to stop in her tracks to rest before continuing her walk. Sometimes she could not walk more than two blocks at a time. Her doctor told her that her pain was the result of a poor blood supply caused by the bad condition of her arteries. This condition, he said, had been caused by her smoking. The name her doctor used for the illness was Buerger's disease. Oh, very trivial!

Since she had been warned that she might risk losing her leg or even her life unless she stopped smoking, I wondered what caused her to be so self-destructive by continuing the habit.

Harriet had made a surface adjustment to life, which allowed her to exist and which she could not afford to question for fear of a total collapse. She had many responsibilities to a wide circle of friends, which forced her to face the world in the role of an efficient, calm, casual, and competent person. Once having set herself up as a public figure, she could not let her "fans" down. She had no choice but to continue to play the part she had created. She would, therefore, find it intolerable to disappoint her admirers and to admit openly a recurrent, vague awareness of her inadequacy. If she were even to talk honestly about herself, she would be brought face to face with a reality she had long avoided. In short, she, who had the power to influence many opinions and who displayed a keen insight into human problems, was blind to her own problems, and to this she reacted with anger and shame.

In reluctantly giving her case history, Harriet, who had just turned forty, revealed that she had started to smoke when she was thirteen years old because, in her own words, "Mother had threatened to whip me if I did." She thought this threat highly unfair because Harriet already supported the family. She explained her childish act of defiance as the result of the unnatural circumstances in which she had grown up.

Harriet was a child actress and traveled with a troupe of adults, all of whom she admired and all of whom smoked. After years of poverty and deprivation, she finally earned a generous salary. This gave her a feeling of adult acceptance at a time when actually she was but a precocious adolescent. Her mother accompanied the troupe as a wardrobe

101

mistress. With their combined salaries they could have been happy and comfortable were it not for her mother's ambition to drive her daughter on to more important parts, which yielded still more money.

Her most vivid childhood memory was being tugged along by her mother from one theatrical agent's office to another, always standing, waiting, walking, being on her feet—remembering how tired her legs had felt and how much she longed to run free. She envied the established actors who came and went as though someone wanted them, and who did not need to walk and wait and stand on one's tired feet for hours. What she longed for most of all was to be with other children.

She could not remember ever playing as a child, only waiting for someone to want her for a part. But she did remember the roles she played, from the bit part at the age of five to child-star roles. She also remembered her mother repeating to her, as her parts became bigger, that God was good to her because she was the instrument to help many people. Mother obviously meant their many relatives and herself, and my patient considered this to be some compensation for her lost childhood.

Educationally, her only break came in Hollywood when, while she was under contract, she had to go to a studio school, as provided by law. "There," she said, "we learned about everything but not very much about anything." Her lack of formal education gave her a sense of inferiority, in spite of her accomplishments.

Her father died suddenly of a heart attack when Harriet was still very young. She never really knew him. Her memory was of "a nice and kind man who drank a lot." Sometimes he traveled with the road company, but not often, and never for long periods. It was her mother who had always been with her. Mother had no respect for father because of his drinking, but later Harriet began to wonder if father had taken up drinking because of mother's rejection of him.

She praised her mother for the love and care she had given her, yet Harriet ventured the opinion that her mother was neither really very gracious nor a good sport. Even when they got good hotel rooms mother would always find something to complain about and, if nothing was done about it immediately, would get very angry and develop a terrible headache to add to her many complaints.

To erase the impression of wanting to be self-destructive, Harriet said that a few times, after the pain in her legs had been terrible and coupled to a sensation that she was going to die right on the spot, she had stopped smoking for a few days. But then a restlessness would come over her, accompanied by a gnawing feeling in her stomach which nearly drove her mad. Her doctor thought she might have developed an ulcer. She underwent X-ray examinations, which showed no lesions, and other tests which did not confirm the diagnosis. The doctor then concluded that her stomach complaints were psychogenic, that her many years of smoking had caused a premature hardening of her arteries, and that this was causing her pain.

Smoking was a compulsive need which she had no power to control. Although the habit had begun as an act of defiance, it had by now become a necessary release of tensions, the only one that gratified her unconscious demand.

We have stated before that the smoking habit answers sexual needs, and if this psychoanalytic tenet is true, it explains a main reason why it is so difficult to break it. When I sought to discover how satisfactory her sexual life was, the patient again responded with initial resistance, but then drew the picture of her husband as one of those rare men who not only never say an unkind word about anyone, but who come to the defense of anyone under criticism. Anything she did was all right with him, and she regarded this as kind and civilized.

But anything her mother did was also accepted by him with equal tolerance. In fact, her husband and her mother had always gotten along splendidly, and sometimes the patient thought that mother was too ready to take his part in one of their rare arguments. When Harriet and her second husband had gone on their honeymoon, mother had gone along because no one had the heart to leave her home alone. Now Harriet wondered why, even if *she* had not had the necessary strength of character, her husband had not opposed this rather unusual situation.

As she released some of her inhibitions and expressed more of her true thoughts, Harriet began to wonder about her mother's control over all that was hers: her career, her household, the rearing of her children, even her husband. All were under the domination of her mother. Her husband's strength was a facade, subtly dominated by her

103

mother. The education of her two sons was controlled by her mother. The home was run by her mother. A busy career had encouraged this, but deeper reasons were to be found in my patient's own passive-dependent behavior.

One day, feeling provoked, Harriet reacted with an unaccustomed anger and she blurted out that she did not like her mother, that she never had. While this was not exactly true, it did describe one most important facet of their relationship. Harriet said she had wondered about this, namely hating her mother and feared that such awful feelings must be abnormal and horrible, because normal girls love their mothers.

After this emotional catharsis she stopped speaking and waited for my comment, as if expecting condemnation or an expression of disapproval. When neither occurred she went on to say that the difficulty with her legs dated back to the family's move from Hollywood to New York five years previously. The move had been spurred by the offer of a television contract which would establish her as the star of her own program on a national network, with a substantial increase in salary. Her husband had been agreeable, she said, stating that in his line of sales work he could do as well in New York as in California. The fact was, however, that under the terms of her new contract, she was making considerably more money than he. He never complained, she said, but it soon seemed that he had lost his ambition to work and quit trying. Although she said that she had wondered about what had caused this change in him, she had demonstrated her custom of evading issues by accepting a superficial explanation. He was seemingly aggressively driving himself through endless luncheon dates and rounds of golf to establish contacts with prospective customers, in order to negotiate his sales contracts. She did not stop to think that he might have been using his luncheon dates and perhaps some extra martinis, as well as those rounds of golf, as escapes from the family.

She had been brought up to please her mother, the audience, and anyone in authority. She had been conditioned to praise the superficial niceties, to be gracious—which meant to be conventionally pleasant in order to be praised—and to be generous for the same reason with little flatteries. She could never be herself. She had learned to be self-effacing. She could never accept failure or admit defeat. Her husband's loss of sexual interest in her she explained as the result of his intense golfing, adding that some men simply release their sexual drive in sports. Even before, she did not have sexual satisfaction, but again she was quick to explain that she did not miss it because she had so many other interests.

But her attempts to explore these other interests were disappointing. The home was run by her mother. When Harriet tried to cook, her mother would come in to the kitchen to supervise and improve. When she realized that her husband was losing his interest in work as well as in her as a woman, Harriet gave up her much-envied job, only to find that now she had no area of activity at all left to herself and that there was nothing she could call her own.

Avoiding introspection because of the frightening self-image she had, Harriet could not see that, while she was completely submissive in one way, in another way she had emulated her mother's domineering, arrogant attitude. She was aware that she really resented and hated her mother, and thought that this was enough to make her abnormal. She has had no other example after which to pattern herself than her mother. But while her mother was a strong, driving, critical and calculating woman, Harriet had only an outer semblance of independence, for inwardly she was crippled. She was a puppet who reacted to the way her mother pulled the strings. Her concern about others and her inner sweetness were borne out of her desperate need to be loved. She tried to be "nice" always and allowed everyone to take advantage of her.

From her mother she had learned to view men as weak, and she was unaware of her own senseless, yet relentless drive to dominate men. She had pitied her father in the same way her mother had when she told her daughter that father had been "a good man except that, poor devil, he drank himself to death."

Were Harriet to realize fully that she was confronted with an intolerable inner emptiness and that her smoking was identified with a childish way of self-assertion, she probably would have collapsed right in front of me. Smoking meant to be grown up but it also was a substitution for a psychic hunger which never had been satisfied. The constant moving during her childhood did not allow her to develop roots or strong ties to people other than her mother. All her life she had played a part and now, after she had given up her job, she had no part to play. Outwardly, she reacted like one of Pavlov's conditioned dogs; she was witty, charming, and generous. And she was nice, always. But inwardly she felt like a helpless puppy. Smoking in her case, as in most cases where it is continued after damage to health becomes evident, was a desperate compulsion to overcome her inner tensions created by her repressed aggression, frustration and her feeling of impotence and helplessness. It did still momentarily some of her inner hunger and it did ease her tensions somewhat. But they never really ceased to plague her because of that secret voice inside her that said that she was a phoney and a colossal failure. The irony in her case was that in the eyes of the world she was considered all that was praiseworthy: an upright, concerned, charitable human being, a talented woman, a good wife and devoted mother who, in spite of her success and the demands made on her, lovingly cared for her old mother. To the casual observer she possessed everything; to the more careful examiner, she had nothing.

Another more recognizable and more problematic escape is alcoholism. I say, "problematic" because the alcoholic, much more than the smoker, escapes reality he cannot accept. While the person who smokes harms primarily himself, the alcoholic who loses control harms others as well—members of his family and the social group in which he lives. We know about the threat the drunken driver constitutes or the dangerous actions or negligence a man or woman can commit in a drunken stupor. Since alcohol has a narcotic effect on the central nervous system which causes an initial exhilaration and a release from inhibition. it is a much-sought-after means of escape.

Alcoholism can cause brain damage and can lead to severe mental disorders marked by a distortion of reality and disturbances of memory. This form of ego indulgence serves as an escape from either a temporary or chronically unhappy reality, and provides for an unreal and brilliant world of imaginary and fantastic experiences. These experiences can sometimes be presented so plausibly that they seem real and factual. Used to excess, alcohol can also produce a variety of physical illnesses and complications, varying from muscular uncoordination to severe damage of nerves and inner organs.

The problem of alcoholism is known in all civilized societies. It is a symptom of man's unhappiness, his inability to cope with life, and the intolerable states of inhibition he experiences as a result of some authoritative control, rejection, hostility, or most often, perhaps, sexual frustration. Even the new social order of the Soviet Union, so greatly advertised as being superior, has not been able to escape this symptom of unhappiness, for at the time I visited that country it had about twice as many alcoholics as the United States.

We must distinguish between social drinking and alcoholism. Social drinking is the occasional or even habitual intake of hard liquor, wine, or beer because of its pleasant effect as a stimulant or relaxer, but an intake which the individual can control as he wishes. By retaining control, we mean that the perceptual senses of the individual are not dulled, that his judgment is not impaired, that he does not knowingly cause himself any physical harm, and that he has the will to stop when he wants to. Alcoholism goes beyond such a point and aims at a state of intoxication which can be acute, periodic, or chronic.

The acute state is a temporary mental disturbance with a decrease in muscular coordination. It is, as a rule, sought in order to bring relief from tension caused by some disturbing or unresolved problem. We are not speaking here about people who, in order to celebrate, take a drink as an acceptable means of escape to increase their pleasure by lowering their inhibitions, unless a pretense is made of celebrating. We are thinking of those people who seek out the warmth and drowsy effect of alcohol to dull an emotional pain, to forget the rawness of an unpleasantness they cannot accept, or to find peace so that they can sleep.

There are dipsomaniacs, periodic drinkers whose intervals of sobriety are followed by another drinking spree, and there is the chronic alcoholic, the morbidly addicted drinker who remains in his toxic state to resist a return to conscious, drab reality.

The motivation for drinking in all three types is a need to seek escape for various reasons and in various degrees. All types imitate, by means of the toxic properties of alcohol, the natural act of protective inhibition, which avoids the injury to brain cells overtaxed by excessive emotions of anger, fear, loneliness, sexual frustration, anxiety about aging or death or other causes of unhappiness. And here we

107

have again an example of the symptom of adaptation turning into a disease of adaptation.

The reasons for seeking escape through alcohol can be understood only in the light of how the individual sees himself and his relation to the world around him. The protective act of seeking a "bracer" for momentary relief from painful tension is, in the chronic alcoholic, an example where a panacea leads to sickness.

I had a patient who, very much like the central figure in a comedy which played in New York many years ago, acted out two types of personalities. When he was sober, he was the conservative, dignified, immaculately dressed executive who carried his briefcase like the symbol of a guild. But when drunk, which as a rule happened when he became upset by some family quarrel, he became careless, merry, and animated, loving the world and everybody around him. He talked to people. He bought rounds of drinks for strangers and was known for his custom of giving enormous tips to a piano player who would play some sentimental song he loved.

This man was behaving like a naughty adolescent who wanted to upset and embarrass his family, especially his pompous older brother, who his mother always held up as the very example of a fine gentleman. But our executive also drank because of his inability to assert himself in his family and because he felt the family never had too high an opinion of him. As a matter of fact the family looked down on him since he had made no success they could be proud of.

What the drinkers of all three groups, at least those I have met in a professional capacity, have in common is a basically low opinion of themselves. Emotionally they are rebels who feel compelled to defy authority by misbehaving and by refusing to play according to the rules of the game, which is to assume a responsible, grown-up mode of existence. Freed from inhibitions, they dare to openly show those feelings they have difficulty in controlling when they are sober. And so, one drinker becomes hostile and belligerent, another becomes affectionate and playful, and still another weepy and suicidal.

I have known writers who drank because they felt that their writing was not as good or forceful or beautiful as they had wanted it to be, or who had felt liquor might eliminate mental blocks.

108

The lowering of inhibition means relief from the rigid world of society and from the individual's own harsh conscience, especially with regard to sexuality. Talk becomes freer, and fear and guilt are cut down to size. Some persons work out their fantasy of self-importance in a drunken state and boast about powers which in reality they would like to possess. Freud pointed out the relationship that exists between alcoholism and homosexuality, which manifests itself not only in men's bars, but in a display of closeness and affectionate feelings which are normally repressed.

Because alcohol animates, and causes giddiness, some people think that it is a stimulant and use it in that sense. But studies have shown that alcohol is really a depressant, and that it lowers mental functioning and memory.

Alcoholics are maladjusted people who feel that they are always misunderstood and condemned, and they expect condemnation even before they are hurt. To a doctor they represent a problem because of their distrustfulness and because they view the doctor as an authority who cannot understand their inner torment, and who is critical and might lecture them about good and proper behavior.

Alcoholism is not inherited. It has its roots in unhappy childhoods, broken homes, or in overindulgent or over-strict upbringings, any one of which can leave a child with conflicts he cannot resolve. Psychologically, what has been said about the oral gratification of the smoker is even truer of the drinker. In addition to its intoxicating effect, liquor satisfies not only those cravings which are centered around the fine nerve endings in the mouth, the lips, and the tongue, but is said to come closest to the pleasantly warming and drowsy effect a baby experiences when, with a fixed stare at his mother, he is sucking her milk. Later in life a lack of security and love makes the potential drinker wish to recapture that period which represented to him the greatest amount of safety and satisfaction he has ever experienced.

A familiar problem with the drinker, as with many other neurotic, compulsive people, is that he denies being an alcoholic. He deceives himself and explains his desire for drink as a social custom or as a stimulant which he needs because of some exaggerated stress. We all have experienced the hospitable urging at a social function to have one for the road so that the host himself can have another drink.

A doctor who came to me as a patient told me that it had

109

taken him a long time to become aware of the secrecy with which he was sneaking drinks. He was convinced that he was handling his liquor well, although his wife had expressed concern about his loud voice, his boisterous manner, and the acerbic arguments he sometimes had with people after he had a few drinks. He denied this for a long time, and he and his wife had heated discussions about it. This went on until one day, when he was with a patient, he drew an agonizing blank and forgot the point he was about to make. He experienced a frightening sense of inferiority and sat helplessly opposite his patient, who was waiting for an answer. The doctor felt that he had at that moment lost his authority and had exhibited a shameful degree of inadequacy. It took him a long time to get over this moment of defeat, and he was dismayed when the memory of the incident returned to plague him from time to time.

When he told me of this incident he could see for himself how fragile his sense of security was, except that he was not sure why certain types of patients should bring back that uneasy feeling and thereby upset him. But he was not sure what types these were. Examining past experiences helped him discover that certain authoritative, hostile personalities had a terribly disturbing or inhibiting effect on him. Whenever he dealt with these people, he was aware that he was not as clear or as forceful as he was with other patients, and he noticed that after seeing such patients the incident lingered on his mind and disturbed him for the rest of the day. This doctor had no doubts about his ability and skill, but he admitted feeling discontented and envious, especially toward those fellow practitioners who were big operators and who charged enormous fees. He tried to console himself by rationalizing that they were probably not very honest men who overtreated and overcharged their patients.

He displayed a considerable amount of defensiveness in examining the area of his self-doubt and the reasons why he submitted to aggressive people, later resenting it and being angry with himself. Unaware of his own particular type of conditioning, he knew only that these incidents in his practice left him with tensions and a hollow feeling in his stomach which he found could be relieved by a quick drink.

His need for a drink was a signal that this man had taken into adulthood attitudes similar to those with which he had met unpleasantness when he was little. His submission to the authoritative people in his environment was the only course of adaptation he could have taken at that time. But now it had grown into a disease of adaptation.

He still submitted to people to whom, rationally, he knew he should not. This caused him to be angry with these people but even more so with himself, the turmoil of which he relieved by the intake of liquor.

As he was able to examine more carefully his responses to people, especially to those who had the power to upset him, he became aware of a need to break his pattern. He found that a tranquilizing drug was not as effective as liquor, but that it nevertheless proved to be a valuable crutch to help him get through the day without the many little defeats and resentments that drove him to drink. And, as is almost always the case, this first step away from a familiar destructive pattern filled him with jubilance and will to undertake the second and third steps of conditioning himself toward a more gratifying, mature life. The surprise and respect his wife displayed proved to be an added incentive in his struggle to rehabilitate himself.

By an alcoholic, we mean a person whose drinking produces a loss of self-control and becomes compulsive even to the point of injury to health and happiness. Such a person can be helped only if he himself decides one day that he wants to stop his drinking and admits that he cannot do it by himself and is willing to accept help.

Such a person came to see me. He was a thirty-two-year-old man who said he had been drinking to excess for almost ten years. He described himself as being accustomed to having twenty drinks a day, and only later confessed that his daily intake of bourbon was two or three times that amount. He admitted that he had fortified himself for this first visit with me by a couple of drinks.

He described himself as always having been nervous, easily upset, distrustful, and very willful. He was an only child, and his early care had been left to a governess while— and he recalled how he had resented it—his parents went out a great deal and travelled extensively. He had been married and divorced, and had two children whom he said he had not seen since his wife moved away.

This caused him, as he said, to drink even more, but the unhappy outcome of his marriage was more an excuse for than a cause of his excessive drinking. After his divorce he

111

found a girl friend, but his disagreements with her—she did not want him to get well, he said—pushed him right back into another drinking bout. He blamed someone else instead of seeking the creator of his obstacles within himself.

There were two basic problems he presented. One was a deep-seated sense of inadequacy which had resulted from his passive, feminine identification. He was afraid of women and had contempt for them, while at the same time he tried to win their favor and be liked by them. The other problem was a state of depression which was nourished by his self-rejection and anger about his wasteful and foolish life.

As a schoolboy his marks had not been good enough to earn him acceptance by any college. He quit one job after another, usually just before he expected to be fired. He went into business for himself and never could quite make the success he thought he should, and each failure filled him with more humiliation. Alcohol helped him to forget these defeats.

So long as he tried to resist his weakness for alcohol the poor fellow was doomed. He was seeking a compensation for his feeling of inadequacy. Alcohol allowed him to forget this need. In order to pull himself out of his rut, he either had to find some other gratification by understanding himself better, or his weakness for alcohol would pursue him to the end of his life. Because of the chemistry of his body or because of the way his body reacts to liquor, such a person can never afford to touch another drop of liquor, not even as a seasoning in food. But if he knows and answers his basic psychic needs, and can understand the reason for his inner turmoil, he may have more will and strength to fight his addiction.

This patient rejected the suggestion that he be hospitalized or that he seek help from Alcoholics Anonymous because he said he had to prove that he could help himself. A few times he came close to what seemed to be a temporary cure, but for some reason or other he never could carry it through. The drug that could help him, temporarily, was an anti-depressant. His deep sense of inadequacy and his repressed anger against authority represented by both parents had caused his depression and made him turn to alcohol as a means of escape. Interestingly, a few months after his father died and his mother, who had always been a tower of strength became ill, he took hold of himself and conquered his addiction.

112

Another patient, who thought that he would not live very long anyway, had increased his intake of alcohol and eventually developed cirrhosis of the liver. He was advised to give up his drinking, although we have learned medically that it is not alcohol that causes cirrhosis of the liver, but a vitamin deficiency resulting from an inadequate intake of food as is the case with most alcoholics.

It was interesting to observe that when this man had anything wrong with him physically, some arthritic pain and, once, pneumonia, he was free from depression, but as soon as the physical illness or discomfort could be overcome, he felt emotionally depressed and sought relief in alcohol.

Often, depressed patients don't know that they are depressed; they only feel that there is something wrong with them, that they feel low and they want relief. A whole group of anti-depressant drugs has lately come into existence because it has been found that states of melancholia are the result of a disturbed enzyme function in the brain, the enzymes being a chemical substance necessary for normal metabolism. These come under the heading of Monoamine Oxydase Inhibitors, called, for short, "MAO Inhibitors." These drugs promise a tremendous step forward in the treatment of mental illness and especially of conditions of depression.

One alcoholic I knew could also have been speaking for my salesman patient when he said that a man must sometimes go down all the way into the gutter, then pick himself up if he wants to cure his alcoholism. This man told how he had lost the vice-presidency of a company and ended, literally, in the gutter. Then, in one sane moment, he was able to see himself and his life in all its misery, and faced the horrible awareness of the dissipated, beaten, dirty and disgusting wreck that he had become. He saw the repugnance with which people made a little detour to avoid being close to him. As he was about to use the dime he begged to "buy a cup of coffee"—which had been his usual plea for money for another drink—he bought a cup of coffee! And from that moment on began a long, difficult, but determined climb back to useful life. He became the president of a big company.

The more than 5,000,000 alcoholics in the United States reported by the National Council on Alcoholism, represent

America's fourth major health problem, along with mental illness, cancer, and heart disease. Alcoholism is a symptom of unhappiness. It is questionable if it can be really separated from a specific manifestation of mental illness. The many explanations given for alcoholism as a result of physiological changes seem to be more symptomatic than basic, and therefore evade facing and working out the real problem. Prohibition, treating ill people like naughty little children, was as we learned, no cure because it only increased an already existing state of rebellion.

Women follow the men. Statistics say there is one woman alcoholic for every 5.8 male alcoholics. Since only 3 percent of the women are the visible skid row types, the problem appears to be less than it actually is. The remaining 97 percent are everywhere—in homes, offices, and factories. They try to live what seem to be normal lives, hiding the fact that they are habitual drinkers. It is estimated that $432,000,000 is lost in wages annually in the U.S. because of excessive drinking, and that this problem costs society more than a billion dollars a year.

Alcoholism is a serious signal of deep and unresolved conflicts, and indicates an individual's inability to make an adjustment between his private standards and those of a hostile society. Because the conflict is so intense, alcohol is the easy escape.

From the point of view of seeking a state of false stimulation or numbness or forgetfulness, drugs, even more than alcohol, are a drastic effort to escape reality.

To stimulate a tired brain or body and to arouse one's senses to keener perception, or to heighten the intensity of pleasure, especially in the area of sex, is one of the oldest and most universal practices by which man has sought to give life an additional thrill or to provide him with an escape from his unhappiness. The need for artificial stimulants documents an unstilled desire and a failure in relating to life positively. It is an escape in that the drug addict feels that life has no real meaning. He sees himself as being lonely, alienated, unable to experience any real gratification, be it in love or work or the joy of sharing genuine feelings with another human being. Fearful, angry, confused, he cannot nor does he want to fit into the society as he sees it and to which he disdainfully refers as The Establishment.

During the past years drug addiction, especially among the youth of America, has come into the limelight of debate. It has been estimated that there are about five million Americans who have smoked marihuana at least once, or pot or grass or weed or mary jane, which are some of the other names used for the drug. The Institute of Mental Health has put the figure closer to twelve million people and believes that a good third of all students in this country have tried marihuana at least once.

Many young people, though considerably less in number, have gone on to more dangerous drugs like hashish ("hash") and heroin. After bewildered parents became aware of the problem, they reacted with anxiety and rage. And many kids enjoyed seeing their original symbols of absolute authority, helpless and confused. The parents turned to their doctors and eventually to the authorities blaming everybody but themselves and then turned their full fury on the criminals for having corrupted their pure and innocent children. The problem grew bigger as the circle of users of narcotics grew wider. Scientists, psychiatrists, psychopharmacologists, politicians and government agencies joined in serious debates about how to stamp out this modern plague.

Initially the question asked was not why the kids were using the drugs but how to catch and jail all the criminals and dope pushers in order to cut off the supply. To many that seemed to be the answer, similar to prohibition after World War I. The Federal Government moved in, set up agencies and committees and controls and stiffened the penalties. Congressional hearings were held, border guards increased, including the showy "Operation Intercept," some time ago, which only alienated and irritated the Mexican Government but proved ineffective. The problem continued to exist.

Why were the kids so eager to reach out for something they obviously were missing—happiness. Some people think that kids are curious by nature and just go for kicks. Yet, not all young people smoked pot or grass (marihuana) or took a trip with LSD (lysergic acid). What then has been causing the seemingly sudden brushfire-like spreading of the use of narcotics—a hunger that essentially is self-destructive? Is it not a hunger for love and a need to be happy? And who is to blame? Criminals? Parents? Parents themselves are often victims of some kind of addictive habit. Kids say that martinis are more habit forming and destructive than pot and readily quote the six million alcoholics in this country, not counting the hidden drinkers. Indeed, pot has not been found to have any serious consequences other narcotics have, unless taken in big doses, but it can help to become a dangerous habit.

Throughout history, there have always been people who have sought escape from intolerable problems or suffering by means of opiates. But there is something different about the youth of today. Whatever the young people may have wanted one or two generations ago in reforms is unmatched by the problems of today's youth. Today's youth does not want to be killed in wars they consider immoral and they don't want to kill other human beings. Today's youth is in rebellion on a worldwide scale because of the threat of nuclear extinction. They unite under the symbol of peace and happiness. Some kids are violent in fighting a rigid authoritative establishment. Others, emasculated by their parents, don't dare to express their anger and appear meek, hopeless and then seek happiness by means of escape, that is, a drug. Others, by joining the hippie movement, seek out an unrealistic make-believe happy group life.

Survival is man's most basic instinct. Kids just don't want any Hiroshimas. They want a right to live and they want a right to be happy, minus the violence they have been watching for years on television.

How the future and happiness of a young man can be destroyed, even when he comes out of a battle alive and with no visible wounds or dismemberment, has been dramatically revealed to me by an incident outside of my office, where I am more accustomed to experiences of human tragedies.

One night, not so long ago, the battery of my car went dead. It was near midnight. I found a garage just at the very east side of Manhattan at the border of Harlem. The traffic had trickled down to only an occasional car passing the open garage. A young man in his early twenties of Italian or Spanish descent by looks and name, was willing to recharge the battery. As he tried to loosen the cables of the battery he suddenly flushed a knife with about an 8-inch broad, rigid blade. I shuddered. "Why don't you use a screwdriver?" "This will do," he replied curtly. After some pause, he looked up and turning the blade, he said, "See this knife—I killed a man with it just the night before last—there were two of them—the other one 'I have' in the hospital—on the critical list." My unease increased. His recharging machine rattled on. "It's self-defense—it's either him or me—I was in Vietnam with the marines—you know, search and destroy mission?—Well, during one of such a mission my brother was killed right before my eyes. I had another brother, also killed—it's always him or me—since then to kill a man means nothing to me—"

"Are you married?" I asked. "Yes, nice wife, nice kids—but I have to live with that terrible thing in me—I am an animal—I know I am—" He offered me and my lady companion chairs and two cokes. There was resignation in his voice when he added, "For the rest of my life I will be an animal—there is no getting away from it—never mind family and all this—I am always on guard—I can kill just like that," and he snapped his fingers. Underneath his casualness this young man had lived with horrors he could not forget and a mixture of rage, guilt and sadness he could not shake.

I believe that when young people take drugs and become hooked, it is not just because of kicks but because they feel lonely, anguished and without close, loving ties. They are unhappy people and seek in some desperate way a substitute for happiness.

Here is a kid sent to me by the family physician. A young man, age 19, was brought into my office by his father, a respectable vice-president of a large company, immaculately dressed. The boy was using all kinds of drugs, cough syrup, "speed" or happy pills. Questioned why he was taking these drugs, he said casually "for kicks." He was a dropout, unhappy and confused. It took several sessions before he began to feel comfortable enough to talk. He was holding a deep grudge against his sister and mother, but more against his sister. "All I think about is to kill her first and then my mother. They make me feel like nothing—like a baby. They snoop. They search my room for drugs. That makes me so mad that each time they say something, I go out and buy more of the stuff (drugs) ." His rage and his obsession to get even with his sister reached at times almost uncontrollable proportions and it was more to get relief from his unbearable tensions that he took drugs. His mother was told in his presence not to enter his room at all and to leave him alone. With tranquilizing drugs and supportive psychotherapy his addiction could be broken. He broke away from friends with whom he had been using drugs. He returned to school and re-established a relationship with a girl who had broken off with him because she did not approve of the gang of boys he was hanging out with.

Narcotic drugs like opium, cocaine, morphine, hashish, heroin and the much milder marihuana, produce an illusion of an excitingly different world, but this is perhaps best understood in the statements of addicts who, after they have been "cured" have told of how empty, cold and disheartened they feel, wondering whether life is worthwhile and whether they should not return to the forbidden but beautiful life of escape.

Many people blame addiction on the acquaintance they made with a narcotic drug after an operation and a wish to return to such a painless state. This is, at best, an act of self-deception. It takes a certain type of personality—most often of the passive and weak-inhibitory structure, with certain types of repressions, mostly sexual in nature, like doubts in one's masculinity, the loneliness of the homosexual and an inward life-denying attitude—to make an addict. Other people experience the effect of a narcotic after an operation or some accident, yet do not feel a need to return to its influence. They can live a life of happiness in reality.

The problem relates to the individual's very basic philosophy, and this is so whether we deal with a case of TB or some other kind of flight into illness, or with an individual who uses alcohol or narcotic drugs as a means of escaping the emptiness of his existence.

The individual who can experience periods of happiness in life will feel little need to numb himself and to deprive himself of the pleasure of natural gratification. Equally, the one who has retained his healthy curiosity and, therefore, experiences delight when he discovers one of the many expressions of natural beauty around him, or who can enjoy the many fascinating expressions of human behavior, wants the true and full and unadulterated experience rather than a neurotic distortion of it.

The drug-addicted patients I have met all along the road of my professional life—artists, writers, or just overgrown childish dreamers—are, deep down, pathetic, melancholic human beings, and it is to the credit of our times that authorities all over the world finally realize that we are

118

dealing with a human problem and not a criminal aberration. Force and threats of punishment have never really resolved problems which are glibly referred to when called "human nature." They only push these problems deeper underground and make them appear in some other distorted way.

Many people believe that humanity has been kept from using violence only because of fear. Personally, I disagree with these people who do not manifest much belief in mankind. This lack of belief may perhaps be a projection of their own neurosis. A mature humanity accepts a rule of law and order because it has learned that the benefits of such a life outweigh the short-lived and destructive passions of a life by force.

Drugs are not unlike the fire Prometheus stole from heaven for mankind. When well guarded, we know that their benefits outweigh their destructiveness. Modern medicine has much to thank in the variety and excellence of the drugs available and being developed, from tranquilizers to vaccines aimed at specific plagues. But some of these are two-edged swords, the narcotics especially, and even the non-addictive sedatives and tranquilizers should be avoided when they threaten to become customary, if not actually habitual, because they permit us to realize a wish to escape reality, and this is a serious signal of deeper, inner trouble.

Not all escapes are as obvious as excessive smoking, drinking, or pill taking. Another much more subtle, but nevertheless destructive escape is overeating. Obesity and bulimia, the insatiable appetite, are symptoms of this type of escape. Medical science has recognized the dangers of overweight and has shifted the emphasis from aesthetic to organic considerations.

In this case, as in others, health is a matter of the balancing of excitation and inhibition. In neurotic states either of these forces may get out of line and diminish the influence of the other. The opposite of bulimia is anorexia. In spite of their need for food, patients suffering from a loss of appetite say that they cannot eat and can become severely emaciated, wasting away sometimes to as little as sixty pounds.

Persons with an obesity problem frequently blame their glands or heredity, or something beyond their own control for their condition. They eat no more than anyone else, they say, and may add, "I eat about as much as a bird." (Yes, a peck at a time.) But we know that there are some people who are as insatiable with regard to food as is the alcoholic in his thirst for another drink.

The wild animal, unlike the neurotic human and his domesticated pet, will not eat more than the calories required to replace lost energy. Even when there is a massive intake of food, as when a snake swallows a lamb, the snake will have no appetite for days after and will make no attempt to eat again, even if a delicious rabbit should present itself.

Pavlov, in his studies of the ordinary, but important food reflex, reported in 1930 the comparison of a normal dog with another in which the cerebral hemispheres had been surgically removed. The normal dog finds his food readily and satisfies his hunger. The dog without the regulating cortex, "as soon as he has exhausted his food supply, wakes up, wanders about and looks for food but cannot find it."

"What happens?" asked Pavlov. "The dog learns at the beginning of his life to locate food by scent and sight, and if the dog, during eating, never saw or smelled the food, then it would be impossible for him to find food by sight or odor." Experiments bear this out. Signals of purpose can become so mixed with the goals, or purposes, that the animal reacts to the signals as if they were goals, like the response to the electric light signalizing food, for example, just as if it were the food itself.

Normal people have a regulating principle for all their bodily functions, including that of needing food. Neurotics, by reason of their neurosis, have lost this regulator. They act like the de-corticated dog, with the loss of awareness of hunger as an indicator for their normal needs. And so we find people who have no hunger but still possess an active appetite.

Psychological investigation has shed more light on the interrelationship existing between an emotional disturbance and obesity. Not only do disturbed people—children and adults—eat out of frustration, they are, it was found, also less active. It is a matter for discussion whether the belief that obesity and sluggish behavior are always caused by inactive glands can be maintained any longer. Sluggishness is frequently due to the lack of mental stimulation or interest or curiosity. And while there may exist a low function of the thyroid or the pituitary, which is the master gland, sluggishness, like boredom, is most of the time an expression

120

of inhibited states. Such states are generally the result of an early conditioning that has led to a repression of unacceptable stimuli.

Specific experiments measuring the restricted activity of obese people have produced convincing evidence of decreased physical activity. Obese women were found to walk less than half as much as non-obese women. That a depressed mental state was causing an inert attitude can be seen by psychological testing at the University of Pennsylvania. In sentence-completion tests—tests in which a patient supplies the finishing half of a given sentence—the difference between obese and non-obese women was vividly demonstrated.

Obese women frequently completed the sentence, "When I'm blue, I . . ." with the phrase ". . . just cry." Non-obese women would say ". . . clean house." Obese women would complete the sentence, "When she's down in the dumps she . . ." with ". . . just sulks." Non-obese women would frequently say ". . . counts her blessings."

The negative, withdrawn, and depressive attitude of obese women contrasted with the positive struggle against the depressive moods in non-obese women.

Because food is turned into energy and because the obese person is not expending the physical energy at his disposal, there is a storing of the surplus in the form of fat. The timid and withdrawn person does not feel driven by active goals, but is content with doing essential work only, hence he is more likely to be fat than the aggressive personality.

Overeating is said to be a substitute gratification for the love and security one may crave but cannot satisfy. A violent craving for sweets in some patients was the result of states of frustration, for which the most frequent causes were found in the areas of sex problems. This may explain why so many people diet and why so many new diets have to be invented. It also may explain why both the diet and the attempts fail, since they do not remove the basic emotional problem.

Here is a story of a thirty-six-year-old woman who used her obesity as a defense against men, marriage, and motherhood. She was a librarian with a college degree who kept dreaming about an independent career, but never dared to take a first decisive step toward it. She was a tall, well-groomed, dark-haired young woman whose chief complaint was her overweight. She did not believe that she was attractive, although most of her friends thought she was. Each time someone complimented her she felt that for one more time she had been able to fool people.

The reason for her coming to see me was that she knew that her weight problem had begun to get out of hand. She felt gross and ugly; she was depressed and discouraged because every time she made an attempt to lose weight the attempt ended in failure.

She was of the type who cry when they feel blue. Being questioned about her life made her burst into tears. She had to struggle against an intense inhibition about revealing anything about herself. Her obesity had troubled her from an early age. She had compulsive eating binges after being upset about something, and each time there followed the agonizing effort of forcing her weight down again.

In describing her ailments, the patient gave me the impression that she believed that she was of an inferior physical quality. Her life was lonely and withdrawn. She had friends; why did she not have a more active social life? She doubted that she had anything to offer them and feared that she would probably bore people. Whenever she was invited to a party she went through a period of turmoil. At first she would accept the invitation, for fear of arousing criticism if she did not, but then she would become upset and try to get out of it. In such evasions she had acquired a masterful skill, but after she had successfully wiggled out of her commitment she was left exhausted, depressed, and feeling even more isolated.

Marilyn, let us call her, had on the surface an appealing personality. This, she said, carried her through the day. But once she reached the safety of her home she felt secure, like the hunted animal who has survived the threats of the hostile world, and there she relaxed and felt exhausted from the struggle to keep up the necessary appearances.

Marilyn always expected to be hurt, somehow. She viewed other people as superior. She considered them more intellectual than she. She envied the ease with which they conducted themselves. She was especially tense when she talked about her father, on whom she blamed all her problems. She described him as a successful businessman who had been an intolerant, autocratic and overly critical disciplinarian. She described what seemed to be a typical incident

122

in their relationship while she was a girl, a scene that lived in her memory almost like a recurring nightmare. It was the breakfast hour. Her heart was beating as she walked down the steps to enter the dining room. Although she kept her glance averted, she felt the sharp disapproving eyes of her father taking in her plump figure. She remembered her agony mounting, and her legs becoming heavy as she walked downstairs, expecting a biting remark or at the least a silent look of reproach. The anticipation of humiliation or rejection every morning filled her with fear, shame, anger, and defiance. There was also a feeling of guilt, which caused a continuous tension that seemed to settle in her stomach.

There were other agonizing memories. Father had built a swimming pool which became a magnetic center of attraction for the young crowd. But what was thought to be a meeting place for gaiety and pleasure turned into a place of unhappiness and a source of trouble for Marilyn. Father began to use the pool to bribe eligible boys to take Marilyn to a dance or social affair. But for Marilyn to put on a bathing suit was a miserable and humiliating struggle. It meant running the gauntlet, exposing her fat thighs to critical spectators, the worst of whom was father. He would ostentatiously praise her younger sister Brenda who, slim and straight, blonde and arrogant, would strut provokingly around the pool.

Marilyn began more and more to invent illnesses as excuses so that she would not have to participate in social functions. But this did not always work. Enraged by her defiance, father would force her out of her room, downstairs, where she stood trembling, only mildly protected by her mother. Unable to contain her inner rage and her feeling that her head was spinning, and not caring anymore what would happen to her, she would storm upstairs again to find release by sobbing in a bed which was warm and a room which was dark. Invariably after such a cataclysm, Marilyn would steal down to the kitchen in the middle of the night to raid the refrigerator. Marilyn wanted to appease her mother by losing weight. She tried it a few times, but somehow she never succeeded. She eventually gave up these hopeless attempts. She resigned herself to believing that her overweight was due to low metabolism, as doctors her mother had taken her to had stated. At only one time, when she left home to go to college, had she lost weight for some unknown reason, finding it not too difficult to diet. But as soon as she returned home, she regained weight rapidly.

Marilyn may serve as an identification for many people who may perhaps have had a different background and different conflicts, but who became obese because food represented a substitute for other pleasures in life which they were too inhibited to enjoy.

To be fed meant to renounce competing for men whom she viewed to be as domineering, cynical, unattractive, and threatening, as had been her own father. To be fed meant to be safe and safety meant the avoidance of hurt and ridicule. Marilyn saw women as being at the mercy of the male sex, and she thought of the sexual act as a humiliating submission.

One young woman patient had made herself ugly and old-looking in order to avoid sexual involvement. Another very attractive girl could not lose weight regardless of how hard she tried because she felt she could not compete with her even more attractive mother; and the more mother criticized her plumpness, the more the girl held on to her protective armor of fat.

Sleep is one more device to which people resort to escape reality. A normal physiological function, necessary for the restoration of the physical and emotional personality, it answers a neurotic need in the withdrawn personality who feels he has nowhere to go, no exciting goals, no meaningful purpose. The eyes of such a personality don't seem to look ahead. They look backward, possibly as far back as the protective cradle or, even beyond this, to the womb—an ideal state of a completely parasitic existence which, since it cannot be recaptured, in terms of wish fulfillment means death.

The function of sleep is in line with Pavlov's theory of protective inhibition. Protracted sleep allows an over-stimulated brain to relax. By avoiding one more dangerous excitation, the cells of the brain can recover.

It is well recognized that sleep is the doctor's aid. There would be much less illness, organic or mental, in the world if people would only heed nature and surrender to the demands of Morpheus. A day in bed can perform wonders in changing a gloomy perspective on life. This recipe is not for all people. The aggressive type will, if forced to stay in bed, become restless and more belligerent, and almost has to be chained to his bed if told to rest.

There are cases, however, when sleep becomes pathological. Sleep is then restless, not refreshing, and accompanied by a mood of depression or melancholy. We all know the leaden drowsiness or need to sleep that comes over us sometimes when we are confronted with a demanding task. If this feeling extends beyond a few days, over an indefinite period, into a desire just to sleep and not to get up to face a new day, a new task, a new defeat, then it is a signal that conflicts may be adversely affecting brain cells beyond their rate of repair and an effort must be made to resolve the conflicts.

Escapes can be healthy or unhealthy, and it is a matter for a sane mind to know the difference. Without some leisure or periodic vacations, the stresses of life—the tiring routine, frustration, or heavy load of responsibility—can diminish energy reserves past the breaking point.

But escapes into sickness, escapes from boredom by providing artificial stimulation, or any other means of persistently evading the facing of an unpleasant reality without making attempts to resolve the disturbance, frequently turn an early neurotic adaptation into a disease of adaptation which constitutes a vast and serious source of unhappiness.

8.

The UNHAPPINESS
Called LONELINESS

SOLITARY CONFINEMENT IS, NEXT TO DEATH, THE HARSHEST penalty man has devised for his fellow man; it is meant to break his spirit while letting his body linger on.

More than seventy years ago, a vernacular and pragmatic William James wrote that:

". . . No more fiendish punishment could be devised, were such a thing physically possible, than that one should be turned loose in society and remain absolutely unnoticed by all the members thereof. If no one turned round when we entered, answered when we spoke, or minded what we did, but if every person we met 'cut us dead,' and acted as if we were non-existing things, a kind of rage and impotent despair would ere long well up in us, from which the cruelest bodily tortures would be a release; for these would make us feel that, however bad might be our plight, we had not sunk to such a depth as to be unworthy of attention."

There are people who live in a state of torment almost akin to confinement because they feel ignored, and they suffer because of their feelings of loneliness. They feel slighted and cut off from the rest of humanity as if they were non-existent. What these people don't know is that they isolate themselves—and worse that if they have an awareness about their self-confinement, they don't know what to do about it or what first step to take to break out of their self-made prison. What holds them back is a sense of being different, of not being wanted and of not belonging. What blocks them, then, is a fear of being rejected and humiliated, all built and snowballed in their own minds.

Feelings of loneliness and isolation are not the same thing as the feeling of "being alone." We can feel lonely in a crowd or at a cocktail party as vividly as we can in solitude feel close to our friends, if they are in our thoughts.

We all may experience moments of loneliness, and this is normal, but the chronic feeling of loneliness from which some people suffer more or less throughout their life is a conditioned reflex, related to the withdrawn-inhibited personality. It has been well established in their personality long before it becomes a serious problem of living.

Love and hate, as said before, are either fused into the one experience of ambivalence or they are twin peaks of emotion, with indifference in the valley between them. Loneliness starts with indifference, a failure or inability to relate to a person or a situation, which compels one to remain aloof. A child is not born with indifference—just the opposite is the case: intensity of feelings and immense curiosity. Indifference, therefore, is a neurotic state. The initial withdrawal may have been a protective act to keep an injured, fragile ego from being hurt; through repetition it becomes an adaptation and, eventually, a disease of adaptation.

In many areas of our lives we support a fragile ego by self-deception. Afraid to face the small, naked real self—we develop techniques of concealing ourselves from others, for fear that revelation might confirm the devastatingly poor image we may have of ourselves. Instead of developing a strong and healthy ego, we keep on, trying to strengthen the admirable facade we have chosen to wear to convince others and, of course, ourselves about our amiability and worth.

I think of a young woman who may perhaps serve as an example of the inability to break through the cordon of restrictions which many of us may have been brought up with. She, as is the case with most of us, could not see herself the way she really was. She was an attractive, chic woman who had reached the peak of her career in her early thirties. Apparently happy and high-spirited, she seemed pleased with herself until about six months before our meeting, when she moved into a new apartment. With a new and important position in her profession, and the new apartment —which was the fulfillment of a lifelong dream because of its prize location, its elegance and comfort—she had attained the pinnacle of her life. Or at least so she thought.

But something strange happened the night after she moved in. She could not sleep. She became frightened; for reassurance she turned on the light in her kitchen. It has burned there ever since. The young woman became increas-

127

ingly nervous, more depressed, and, what was more bewildering, she lost interest in her work. She found it increasingly difficult to get out of bed each morning, and began to rely on alcohol to get through the day and to sleep at night. She began to look ill. One day an old friend met her and, shocked by the drawn and dissipated expression on her face, brought her into my office.

This young woman realized that she had fulfilled the ambition of both of her parents. She also realized that she had sacrificed marriage and children, putting these things off, "just for another year," and another, when she would be even more desirable by getting where she wanted to be in her career. She was driven by an unconscious need to please her mother, although her mother had never expressed in words any ambitious goals.

This patient, as a girl, had picked up her mother's fantasies of grandeur. Now that she had "succeeded" and nothing in her life had changed, the young woman experienced an immense letdown, a crushing feeling of disappointment and futility. Suddenly she felt immensely lonely. All her life she had waited for the moment when something wonderful was going to happen, once she had proven herself successful in the eyes of the world. This expectation drove her on and on. She had never stopped to explore rationally her eventual goal. She was shrewd in matters of business and a child in her emotional judgement. Ever since she had left college she pursued single-mindedly her career, motivated by a need to win one more victory and success would be hers. She was certain that once she would reach the peak of success the long-hoped-for recognition, with an exciting award, would finally come to her and that then she would be happy.

In her mind she had associated success with some uncertain, entrancing award—actually, the special and deserved love of her parents—and it was this desire which pushed her on. But what she failed to recognize and needed to know was that happiness comes from within and that true success comes in acceptance of oneself as a first step to maturity. Seeking praise for her superior marks in school and in college had made her an instrument for the ambitions of her mother who, because she had lacked the education for a career, lived out her ambition through her daughter. The girl's intense studies had isolated her from friends. It had prevented her from forming trusting relationships and from enjoying herself with the abandonment of youth in having dates and romantic involvements.

Examination of the motivations for her drives and actions made her see that all along she had been pleasing her bosses and everybody in authority as she had been accustomed to pleasing her parents. When she moved into her new apartment, she had reached her goal. There was no further incentive to drive her on. All of a sudden, as her race came to a stop, she felt overcome by a colossal sense of failure. She struggled in vain against a vague realization that as a human being and as a woman she had lived an unfulfilled life. She had never allowed herself the luxury of leisure; she had never had any time to waste. Her interest had been her office and her work. Now she questioned whether this interest had not, from the viewpoint of achieving happiness, meant a waste of her life.

My questions disturbed her because she had asked some of them herself and had evaded the answers for so long. It was in my office that she experienced the cruel realization that she had not lived an independent existence at all, but one of enormous pretense and that she had performed like a puppet, seeking approval from everybody and denying herself any affectional involvement or gratification of her own human needs. The moments of satisfaction she had experienced when she climbed another rung of her professional ladder were short-lived and not sufficient to still the emotional hunger which remained unsatisfied and had kept her moving. Now, her many repressed angers and resentments were beginning to break through her diminishing self-controls. She tried to stem them with the aid of alcohol and by the regressive act of not wishing to get out of bed.

To women, the mid-thirties seem to be their second period of crisis. Different from the first critical years when a girl becomes a woman, and is confronted with the need to accept her womanhood and to make decisions about assuming her role as a wife and mother, and also different from the time when the hormone-glandular system changes and the menopause signifies the physiological end of her childbearing period, the mid-thirties, at least in our society, suggests a last warning to a woman that if she wants another child, this is the time to have it. Although a woman can conceive as long as she menstruates, women after their mid-thirties consider themselves, as a rule, too old to bear children. Also, for women who have had children, the mid-thirties are years of transition, for their youngsters are becoming teenagers, who now strive for more independence and who make fewer demands on their mothers. The problem for the mother then arises of what to do with her time and energies. For women who have not had children or who have not married, the years of the mid-thirties are grim reminders that they have missed what might be called a "woman's destiny." Consequently, the mid-thirties are years of intense problems and of frequent breakdowns.

One such woman came to see me because a co-worker of hers, who herself had gone through a terrifying experience, had recognized the ominous flicker in this woman's eyes and insisted that she seek help without delay.

This woman, Mary, kept her composure with difficulty. Though thirty-six, she was much younger looking. It was obvious that she was uncomfortable talking about herself, and she struggled painfully to keep her self-control. She said she had always prided herself on being self-sufficient, and she believed she could work out her own problems. But her life seemed to have become unbearable and meaningless. When I asked her if she knew why, she answered, "Because of loneliness."

This term set off an emotional explosion, culminating in statements like, "All my life I have been lonely" and "Thousands of nights I have cried myself to sleep feeling alone, ugly, and unwanted. I just don't want to go back to that."

She told me that she had developed a pleasant, easygoing, gregarious facade which served as a social shield to the world but which never allowed her to forget that deep down she was alone. "Now, at my age, I am sick of acting. Life is passing me by, and I am frightened. I am frightened of the dead feeling of boredom and of the long, lonely hours, with an expanse of longing and unfulfilled hope. It is worse than any illness."

Why had she waited until she was in her mid-thirties before being able to get involved in a serious relationship with a man? Her comment on this subject was a sharp and sarcastic, "Where do you find a man? On the subway? On the street? In your backyard?" She gave rational explanations of how she had been unable to meet men: that there were no eligible men in her office; that she had gone to a women's college; that most attractive men were married, while the rest were "fairies."

When a person is hungry he knows, somehow, how to get food. If a woman says that she does not know where to meet men, either her need is not very great or else the fear which inhibits such actions outweighs the need. Such a woman is not really making a serious effort.

When we speak of loneliness, we should distinguish between loneliness, aloneness, and unpopularity. Shyness, introspection, introversion, found in people of a rather cold temperament who like to be alone and don't want to be bothered by other people, is characteristic of the withdrawn-inhibited personality. Because the behavior of such persons resembles certain aspects of schizophrenia, they are called schizoid personalities. These people may have a smooth, inconspicuous, even attractive social ease, but deep within themselves they remain uninvolved.

Another type of loneliness is that of people who do not want to be alone, but who, like frightened children, don't know how to go about being more social and gregarious. On the surface they appear to be aggressive personalities, and often by this very aggressiveness and nonchalant behavior they defeat themselves. Their aggressiveness is an overcompensation for their sense of inferiority. It is this defense, and the fear of being found inadequate and of then being rejected which causes them to stay away from other people or to remain uninvolved. This kind of loneliness seems to be a growing social problem, especially in big cities where modern times have changed old-fashioned, neighborly conduct into one of little concern for one's neighbor next door, who one may hardly know. A similar loneliness seems also to be a problem among the older generation. People who retire, or become widowed, or because of their lessened or lost earning power have to move, and find themselves estranged and often, because of a feeling that nobody likes old people, proudly keep away from others.

Mary belonged to the second group of lonely people. She desperately desired to be part of a group, to be liked, and to belong. At the same time, however, she felt inadequate. Her father had been crippled when Mary was a schoolgirl and thereafter lived as a recluse in the attic. She was very much ashamed when other girls talked about their daddies. She was embarrassed that their family was poor and lacked any social importance. She had aligned herself with her mother, who, she knew, had hated her father for his inability to take care of the family.

Mary had not had the example of an inspiring and happy home, or a forgiving mother, or a concerned father. She grew up to see women as carrying an undue amount of responsibility, and to see men as unreliable and untrustworthy. It is understandable that she could not feel excited by the thought of rushing into an institution that was as unrewarding as she had known marriage to be in her own home. On conscious levels, Mary defended herself against her feelings of being deprived by telling herself that she wanted to get married but just had to wait until the "right" man would come along.

Mary's attitude towards sex was also influenced by her mother's ascetic feeling about all that related to lust and pleasures, and she learned at an early age to repress severely her sexual needs. She compensated by an emphasis on intellect, and she prided herself on being bright and quick-witted, only to find that intellect was of no use to her when she was confronted with her own problems and confusions.

Being self-conscious of her age Mary stood at a crossroads. What was the deeper nature of her Gordian Knot? Mary had buried deep in her mind the warm love which she had had for her father when she was little, something she had forgotten and successfully covered up by her resentment of him. By rejecting him, she rejected all men as undependable and inefficient. She was not even aware that her conversion to Catholicism was symbolically an affront and a rejection of her mother's Presbyterian faith, and that by embracing her father's religion she meant to embrace him and find him.

Mary had not cut the tie with her father and therefore could not grow up to meet reality realistically. As long as she was searching for her father, who would take care of her, she would remain the child she once was, who had been cared for. She did not want to grow up, for growing up meant to be like mother, strict, undesired, unhappy, and alone. Lacking a clear concept of what a mature man-woman relationship is, she had emulated her mother and had developed a conditioning like that of her mother, while deluding herself in the belief that she was different. The mere resentment of mother's way of dominating and belittling men did not help her behavior toward men. Mary was not conscious of her unresolved conflict, which was either to be like mother—hostile toward men—or to remain a

132

child, hoping to obtain the care and comfort of a child, which was, of course, unrealistic. But not knowing this made her continue her ungratifying existence, which could be resolved by her finally making the long-postponed decision to cut the neurotic ties which held her down and to make a mature adjustment to her situation.

Our first patient, who in her luxury apartment felt so overwhelmed by the dead oppressive stillness of her loneliness that she had to use alcohol to gain oblivion from her sense of vacuity, was quick to realize how the chase of parental rainbows had isolated her from life to such a degree that she feared madness and was so frightened by ghosts that, like aborigines who try to frighten away evil spirits by fire, she kept the light in her kitchen burning.

"I have spent the loneliest and most miserable Christmas ever," she said one day after she had realized her problem. "But I refused to go home because I thought, if I don't break my pattern of dependency, I will lose my chance forever."

Within three months she was married, saying that her choice was a man who came closer to fulfilling her own standards than the lofty ones she thought her parents expected of her.

The second woman was not able to make a decision so readily. There was an elaborate defense system consisting of a fear of men, a fear of sex, and a fear of abandonment and hurt that had to be resolved before this woman would dare to cut the ties which had provided some sense of security. Some people dare to act, and others, out of fear, prefer the safety of their seclusion.

Loneliness may be a first symptom of an underlying depression. It may be a neurotic state or a more serious symptom of mental illness.

Lonely people are unhappy people. They are people who have grown up with a degree of inhibition so great that not only has it extinguished the spontaneity of a joyful life, but it comes dangerously close to that state of absolute inhibition which is death.

These people need help, but this is often made difficult by their inhibition to expose themselves and their misery. If we understand the dynamics involved we can help ourselves. Or we can help some other lost soul who like a longing child is watching other children play, needing and hoping for encouragement to take the first positive step out of isolation. The line that separates us all and causes many of us to suffer unnecessarily from loneliness, let us remember, is a fluid one.

9.

SIGNALS and
COUNTERSIGNALS

"MAN CAN DO AS HE WILL, BUT NOT WILL AS HE WILL,"
Schopenhauer said, thus expressing the very essence of the
ancient question of man's free will. Is man a free, responsible being or is he a pawn of fate? Does he chart his own
course or is he pushed by an inexorable destiny which he
cannot escape? If reflexes act for us instantaneously, without troubling to ask us for a conscious choice of alternatives,
and if firmly established adaptations move us before we
have that brief pause to consider the wisdom of a response,
then how can we ever expect to really know what we are
doing? Moreover, how can we truly exercise any rational
control over ourselves?

And yet, the very knowledge of the power conditioned
reflexes have over us, and of how they can be understood
and changed, delivers man from his superstitions and fills
him with the confidence that, within the given framework of
nature and its reality, he can truly chart his own course
toward his self-chosen goals.

But first, we must have objectivity about ourselves. We
must know what we want to do and what we can do, that is
we must realize our potentials as well as our limitations
within the framework of reality. Toscanini, considered the
leading conductor in the thirties and forties, admitted to
a friend that when he realized that his compositions would
never equal those of Beethoven, decided to become the
world's greatest conductor, and he did.

We must want individual independence, so that we dare
to assert ourselves in the many give-and-take interpersonal
relationships, for this is how we find happiness in the home
we build and in the work we do. And we must want to
accept the responsibilities of an adult life if we want to

fulfill ourselves as adult human beings. This is how man has carried forward the torch of truth and progress in all he has created, as an individual or in a teamwork towards an unknowable infinity.

In our everyday existence we often struggle through a maze of confusion because we lack the clarity and the ability to act—even if we possess the objectivity about a problem—because of the resistance of a powerful system of conditioning.

A woman who was very unhappily married had finally come to understand the nature of her problem. She believed the problem to be the uninvolved attitude of her husband, who seemed to have no awareness or even an interest in learning what was wrong between them.

"How can I make him see the problem?" she asked. And her question might be extended to asking how any one of us can see life as it truly is, and see it whole, especially in a close relationship with another human being. Our subjectivity, our discontent, our unhappiness and wishes for something else, blind us to reality. There is the danger that we may get lost in pursuing vague and distant goals, and forget the plain facts and the needs of each ordinary day. However, if we know where and how to look for them, there are signals which can help us to an objectivity about the nature of the world around us, about our own position, and beyond this can guide our responses in the direction in which we want to go. But first it is necessary to recognize the signals which set off specific chain reactions and lead to neurotic responses. We therefore must learn how to replace our signals, established in us by our first conditioning, with new, maturer or more desirable countersignals. Since we react to the ring of the Pavlovian bell in exactly the same way as to the original piece of meat, we can, instead of dreaming about the meat, associate the two signals, then dismiss the bell for the meat we desire—the love, the acceptance, or the successful conclusion of a project we desire.

In Chapter 4 I told the story of the lawyer who fought the image of his autocratic father in the person of the judge. The uncontrolled temper which led to his disbarment caused him and his family great harm and unhappiness. The signal in the lawyer's unconscious mind was:

"I am angry because I was dominated and beaten down by an intolerantly strict and inconsiderate father, and I didn't like it. I don't have to take this abuse anymore. I am

136

strong now. I can dare to rebel, and I am going to tell him off! That will help my injured self-image and make me act like a man, and that is what I must do, always!"

And so, he fought his father in the person of the judge, provoking the latter in a vain effort to heal an old, smarting wound. It was his neurotic attempt to cure a pain that had occurred a long time ago, by acting out the way he had wanted to act toward his father but did not dare. And so, the pain had lived on in his mind unresolved and readily inflamed.

After recognizing the uselessness of this struggle, the lawyer had to create a countersignal, which went something like this:

"I am a grown man now, and nobody can dominate me unless I allow it. The judge is not my father. Therefore, if I defeated him, I still wouldn't wipe out the old pain; I still wouldn't gain the satisfaction I so urgently desired when I was a boy. I am distorting time, place, and situation when I provoke the judge, and he will respond with hostility. I will pick up his anger, adding it to mine, and I will then react with a blinding inner rage. Then I will lose control and he will gain power over me, just as father did. My fight does not free me, but brings about precisely what I had tried to overcome. I must therefore not lose my independence as a grown man, and I must not hand it over to another."

Similarly, the young research economist referred to earlier had changed her job. This had meant an increase in prestige and salary, but there was one problem which wore her down and increasingly began to inhibit her: her boss. She possessed sufficient perception to realize that she reacted to him as to her own father, a cold, critical, and cynical man who always managed to leave her shattered. She did not act out as the lawyer did; she became depressed.

"I tried to say to myself, he is not my father, but I still react in the same old destructive manner."

She was basically passive, dependent. She was of a type that is afraid to lose control, and like some people who fight an anesthethic this woman unknowingly resisted her new signal. She proceeded, we may remember, by reliving a thumbnail version of the conditioned reflex itself:

"I must associate my boss with kind old Uncle Henry," she said to herself. "Uncle Henry, under his grim facade, had a heart of gold and was full of love. I must think of Uncle Henry every time I meet my boss."

Some time later she reported how successful this approach had been. At first she had attempted to free herself by trying to remember that her boss was not her father. It did not work. The new association of Uncle Henry with her boss, the replacement of a "threatening" signal with a "kind" one, was Pavlov's principle in reverse. In this way she could become more and more uninhibited or, if we continue our associative reflex game, she could by dismissing the bell obtain the meat, which for her meant obtaining secure behavior, a secure position, acceptance, love, etc.

The rebellious lawyer accepted a signal more readily because of his outgoing and more optimistic temperament, while the young woman was slow, because she was a more pessimistic and resistive personality.

We often use this device intuitively, as in the case of a woman who had a problem of being aroused sexually by her sluggish husband. "The only way I can make love with him she said is to associate him with Gregory Peck, and in my mind to have a love affair with the actor." This kind of speech to oneself needs drill to create a new signal. Enough drill can make the automatic response unfailing, even though the signal may be in opposition to all the things one has been brought up to believe and do.

That such an approach has a scientific basis can be seen in an experiment in which the researcher conditioned the pupillary reflex so that it would react to the command "contract." First, an associative reflex had to be established between a light and a sound by repeating the sound each time a light struck the pupil. Later, the patient said "contract" each time the sound was made. Eventually, no sound was necessary; the mere word "contract" was sufficient to produce a contraction, which still later was obtained by only thinking of the word "contract."

There are similar experiences of hypnosis or self-hypnosis in which a properly prepared command produced a state of relaxation which could not be produced by simply willing it. Empirically, military basic training has used this method to make upright young men react automatically to a given command to kill without hesitation, in spite of any and all previous training to the opposite. Some of these men who had been in battle were forced after the war to unlearn their newly learned reflex.

Because a conditioned reflex is automatic, we have no time to make a speech to ourselves, as did the lawyer I described. Also, because signals are specific, they must pertain to the newly desired response. Moreover, signals must be short and precise. A process of chain reactions take place between impulse and action. A well-planned signal can intercept a response before the wheels start going in their automatic rotation and turn them into another more desirable direction.

The lawyer was disbarred for his repeated displays of uncontrolled temper and was then obliged to turn to tax work for a livelihood. But he continued to have violent altercations with his business associates, and this was a first signal to him. It called to his attention that he would soon find himself turned out of a second profession unless he changed his conduct.

This signal of alert was enough to intercept the automatic response. Next, another signal was needed to restore his self-control. He prepared for this in advance by making speeches to himself. The signal he devised for emergency use was the brief sentence: "You are not my father. I don't have to rebel." He said it to himself whenever he felt himself about to respond to a feeling of disquieting injustice, and he found the signals helpful in gaining a new more realistic view of a situation.

To be sure, the first conditioning is a powerful one, so powerful that it is never fully erased. Reconditioning is like forming a new circuit in the brain, with new responses. Sometimes under great stress, impulses may be thrown back to follow the old route. I remember, during my first years of practice in New York, a scene with a patient who was a young and beautiful model. After her problem had become clear to me, I tried to explain her situation. She listened with utmost attention, but when I concluded and paused, she said, "Now, would you be good enough to repeat what you have just said in English?" I was totally unaware that I had been speaking in German, which had been my first conditioning in speech and thought, and to which I regressed under the immense stress of the European war that had just broken out and the anxiety about members of my family caught in the inferno.

The choice of countersignals is as varied, of course, as the situations for which they are needed. The young lawyer who could not get a job except the one he did not want in his father's office was able to stop himself from responding in his old manner by saying to himself, whenever he felt intimidated in an interview, "You are not my mother and I am not a little boy anymore, 'I am a grown man and must behave like one.' " This was enough to give him some perspective and something to hold on to. With that little bit of support he could cope with the situation more on its merits rather than the blind response of his previous conditioning.

A woman who was a talented painter felt utterly frustrated by her inability to draw. With color and composition she produced imaginative effects, but the lines she drew were those of a child. Her problem was that she could not settle for anything mediocre. Whatever she attempted had to turn out to be a masterpiece. Her frustration and undeserved sense of failure were causing mental and physical disturbances in her. But a speech to herself in which she said, "Move forward; be content with one little step at a time, and worry about your masterpiece later," helped her to break her impasse. She was able to resume work because she could be content with advancing by small degrees. There are as many variations to the theme of creating new signals as there are neurotic responses to life situations provided we have gained enough insight about our self-defeating behavior and provided we are determined to change.

An unhappy young woman, whose financé had left her and who felt deeply depressed and suicidal, could remind herself that she was following her old melancholic trend of withdrawing and feeling sorry for herself by giving herself over and over the signal, "Stop your regression!" and do something, anything.

A famous Hollywood star felt driven relentlessly and unhappily to wipe out of existence the painful rejection she had suffered from her father. Her very notable achievements in her career were never satisfying to her until she understood what she was trying to do. Then the signal, "I don't have to prove anything to anyone anymore; I can allow myself to relax and enjoy what I have and who I am!" was a helpful first step to break some of her tensions. It did not quickly cure the conditioning but it helped to ease her inner restlessness and permitted a reconditioning of her immature and wasteful neurotic drive.

"Keep smiling" and "Every day in every way I am getting better and better!" are or had been familiar slogans. Actually, they are signals intended to trigger our conditioned

140

responses in the right direction, but the reason they fail is that these slogans disregard the complexity of our conditioning. A thin surface smile cannot remedy deep inner turmoil, or frustration, or anger, or hopelessness.

It happens very often, though not always, that these signals relate to some intricate parental relationship; domination by a mother, overindulgence, or rejection by a father or the other way around. Perhaps a child strives to win from a parent the affection he feels he never got but believes was given to a more favored brother or sister. What matters is not what precisely the set-up had been but how the growing up child perceived things to have been. The mother of a young female teacher told me that she may have neglected her child. But please understand, said the mother, "There was a depression and I had to worry about things." An absurd statement indeed!

The nature of the relationship between child and parent is so complicated and the neurotic effect parents have on their children so unintentional, that they cannot be blamed. In most cases the parents are not aware of the destructive effect they have on their children. Indeed, most parents do the best they can. Where they are less than perfect the fault lies at least in part with their own parents, and thus goes all the way back to Adam and Eve. Because it begins at the start of life, the parental relationship exercises the most profound influence on the making of the young personality. Unhappy events being forgotten, it affords clues to the discovery of specific conflicts in later life. Even where the child-parent relationship is a justified cause of one's unhappiness later on, to blame the parent is only to compound the damage. We keep on hurting ourselves. But by understanding the causes of our unhappiness and by attempting to recondition our responses, we can cure self-destructive and morbid behavior.

Signals may serve two purposes. They may be used to deliberately trigger a response that is considered desirable, or they may call attention to conditions which our subjective minds are otherwise unable or unwilling to recognize. Certain illnesses seem to be signals useful to this second purpose.

The Chicago Institute for Psychoanalysis, under the distinguished and imaginative direction of Franz Alexander, has conducted a ten-year study of seven diseases which would seem to have specific relationships to psychic causes:

duodenal or *peptic ulcer, ulcerative colitis, bronchial asthma, hypertension, neurodermatitis, arthritis,* and *thyrotoxicosis*.

The patient who suffers from a *duodenal ulcer* shows as his dynamic problem a frustration of his dependency needs. The childish craving to be fed appears later as a wish to be loved, which can be symbolized in a need for constant support—advice, money, gifts, etc. The standards of an adult man or woman are often in conflict with these needs, and result in hurt pride and unhappiness. Many people of this type defend themselves against this dependency by over-compensating and become "go-getters," hoping thereby to attain their need to be loved and comforted.

People who suffer from *ulcerative colitis* have lost hope of being able to accomplish a task that involves responsibility, effort, and concentration. When confronted with obstacles, these people tend to lose hope easily, and they often lose their confidence as they move toward some achievement. Many were found to have been exposed in early childhood to challenges which were beyond their capacity. Ambitious parents have in some way expressed great expectations for their child, and the child now feels that he must perform in order to secure mother's love and acceptance.

The patients who suffer from *bronchial asthma* show that they had been threatened with the loss of their mother's or a mother substitute's attachment. When a child felt the growing force of his sexual strivings, he lived with the fear of alienating his mother's attention. Later in life this fear becomes evident, frequently in long engagements but an inability to marry, which would result in the child's losing the love of his mother or of feeling the wrath of mother's disapproval. A girl may suspect a mother's unconscious jealousy, with the result that she experiences a conflict between her sexual needs and her fear of her parent's disapproval. An outstanding feature of these patients has been their conflict about crying. Most of these patients have felt inhibited about crying for fear of maternal rejection. Asthma attacks are explained as an inhibited use of the respiratory tract for communication, a substitute for crying or confession. The common allergic disease, hay fever, is a minor form of asthma.

Patients suffering from *hypertension* have been found to be engaged in a continuous struggle against expressing their hostile-aggressive feelings, with a consequent difficulty in asserting themselves. Such people are afraid of losing the affection of others and therefore attempt to control the expression of their hostility. As children, most of them were found to have been prone to attacks of rage and to have been aggressive, but then, at some point, a change of attitude had taken place, either suddenly or gradually. The aggressive child cannot assert himself and becomes overly compliant. These people as a rule show a dogged perseverance in pursuing their tasks against formidable obstacles. In their work they have job records of long standing, staying with a company even when they are poorly paid and when they inwardly resent it. They burden themselves with excessive work loads and responsibility, often without adequate compensation, and get deeper and deeper in a vicious circle of being weighted down by responsibility on the one hand and repressing their hostile feelings about it on the other. If such a person becomes an executive, he is said to find it difficult to assert himself and to delegate work. He will often rather do the job himself than let his subordinates do it.

Neurodermatitis, a group name for skin disorders due to disturbed states of nerves, has been found in those who experience a conflict between their exhibitionism, guilt, and masochism, combined with strong needs for the physical expression of love from others. The researchers found that these patients as a rule have had undemonstrative mothers who created in the child a great hunger for that type of skin stimulation which goes with the physical expression of love on the part of the mother. They want to be stroked and cuddled. In general, there was a lack of close physical contact, and the need for this was never sufficiently satisfied in the early part of their lives. These patients try to get attention by means of infantile exhibitionism, similar to that which induces adults to cuddle children.

The early exhibitionistic techniques are aimed at attracting the parent's attention away from either the other parent or a sibling. If the attempts succeed, they cause a feeling of guilt, which manifests itself in a tendency "to put the wrong foot forward," to appear "in a bad light," to make embarrassing faux pas, to make "fools of themselves." The sexual impulses in these patients, in which the skin eroticism is accentuated, are deeply linked with guilt feelings. Neurodermatitis, the doctors found, is precipitated after the patient achieves some form of exhibitionistic victory. The victory arouses guilt and creates a need for suffering precisely

143

on that part of the body which was involved in the exhibitionistic success. By scratching, which psychoanalysts explain as a substitute for masturbation, the patient removes both the sexual tension and at the same time inflicts pain upon himself. Some patients vividly describe the pleasure they derive from scratching. They refer to it as a "vicious" kind of pleasure, and in these orgies of scratching they attack their body mercilessly and experience pleasurable pain, or painful pleasure.

Arthritis seeks out more women than men. Patients suffering from arthritis, similar to the hypertensive patients, were found to have great difficulty in handling their aggressive-hostile impulses, but differed from the hypertensive patients in combining self-control with a benevolent tyranny over others. It was found that women who have suffered from arthritis, when they became mothers, showed compulsive tendencies and an inclination to closely control all the activities of their children, demanding their participation in the daily chores of the household. In their own childhood, it was found that these women had been exposed to similar maternal influences. The typical mother of the arthritic patient is said to have been a restrictive one. Their punishment has been, mostly, a deprivation of their physical freedom. Young girls, before they menstruate, often react to such physical restriction by becoming tomboys, competing with the boys and fighting with them. This kind of muscular activity is said to have been highly eroticised, and in that way the pent-up rebellion was drained away. Later in life, the tomboy expressions of rebellion are transformed into a tendency to tyrannize others. The feeling of guilt is minimized because the tyranny appears to be helpful. Such a person is strict but takes care of the interests of the submissive. The researchers found that in men feminine identification existed, against which they defended themselves in a way similar to women.

It is said that arthritic conditions frequently develop when the drainage of hostile impulses by ruling and helping at the same time is blocked by a change in the external life situation. The loss of a person who was dominated can be a precipitating factor. Repeatedly, the disease is precipitated when a husband or child makes a successful attempt to stand up to the domination. The interruption of the physical outlet is also said to be a precipitating factor, because it increases the inner tension.

144

Thyrotoxicosis is a morbid over-functioning of the thyroid gland. People suffering from such a disease are said to live in a constant struggle against fear. This fear is related to the physical integrity of the body and manifests itself specifically as a fear of death. Many of these patients try to master this fear by denying its existence, and by contraphobically seeking out "dangerous" situations and coping with them by relying only on themselves. The case histories of these patients reveal frequent exposure to death in near relatives, or other traumatic events which they interpreted as a threat to their own survival. They are said to have dreams about dead people in coffins, and the precipitating situation is some threat to survival. An acute state of thyrotoxicosis is said to follow immediately upon some traumatic event such as an accident, a condition which physicians refer to as "shock-Basedow," Basedow being the name of the German physician who first described this disease. Only careful and methodical scrutiny can bring to light the threatening event which immediately preceded the outbreak of the disease.

Another characteristic is said to be that these patients have matured rapidly. The example was given of a motherless, six-year-old girl who cooked for the whole family and acted as a little mother to her younger siblings. But only predisposed individuals are said to respond with thyrotoxicosis. The predisposition is given not only by heredity and constitution, but also by the type of life history in which threats to mere survival have repeatedly occurred.

It is probable that all our organic ailments, if we understood them well enough, would give us clues to our psychic disturbances just as an understanding of our psychic conflicts would give us a clue to acute or recurrent organic ailments. We still lack the full knowledge of the delicate interaction in the field of psychosomatic medicine, especially in the area of tissue changes, tumor formation and premature aging.

We have sufficient and steadily growing evidence that emotional turmoil can cause a specific illness which clears up when the conflict is resolved or abates.

We know for instance that many people suffer from an allergy called hay fever, and we have learned that a suppressed desire to cry is the psychic origin of this kind of ailment. But we also know that crying now won't cure it. The trouble began long ago, when the sufferer was a small child. Knowing something about the nature of its origin

145

can help us to begin a process of reconditioning of the personality which may end conditioned responses and relieve the suffering. In the long run it may ameliorate, if not completely alleviate the condition.

While I was a young assistant my medical chief left some patients in my charge while he was on vacation. One was a middle-aged woman who suffered from asthma attacks. Because she was wealthy, she had been sent to practically all the leading authorities all over Europe. The painted walls of her bedroom, termed a cause of her allergy, had been ripped out and replaced by wood panelling; later this was replaced by silk, then by special wallpaper. An allergy-free chamber was built—this was before air conditioning—to prove that she was allergic to some as-yet-unknown agent in the air. Indeed, during the testing she had no attacks but, since she could not live in a chamber, she was advised to go to Switzerland. While there, she felt well. As soon as she returned to her home, however, her attacks returned, and they were so severe that she was urgently advised to go back to Switzerland.

This time the charm did not work, and she came home physically exhausted and despondent from her many attacks. It was at about this time that I saw her. At that time, psychological factors as a possible cause of disease were considered farfetched. Nevertheless, in talking with the patient I obtained some information about her personal life. I learned that during her first stay in Switzerland she had been alone and had felt relaxed, while during the second visit her very worried husband had gone with her. Knowing what little was then known about the psychic conflict which is now assumed to be a cause of asthma, I told my chief that I thought this woman was allergic to her husband, not to some imagined poison in the walls of her bedroom. He dismissed my diagnosis as amusing but very unscientific. It turned out, however, that the attacks were indeed provoked by tension between the woman and her overprotective husband.

As I understand it now, to get well this woman had to be brought face to face with her problem that she did not really like her husband while at the same time was enjoying the good life he could provide for her. She had to make a decision to either leave him or to stay with him. In the latter case she had to make compromises and accept him the way he was rather than to act like an innocent child denying her negative feelings toward her husband and blame her state of stress on the paint of her walls or some other mystical toxic agent for her discontent (illness). While it is true that some specific irritant can trigger off a chain reaction and physical symptoms, like allergies, this woman reacted to the signal of dislike (her husband) by not leaving him but by repressing her true feelings (resentment). Instead of the normal response of fight or flight which would have solved her problem she made herself oblivious to the reality and remained in conflict. The ensuing tensions were being misdirected into a negative stalemate battle, which psychosomatically produced the morbid picture of her asthma attacks.

The reconditioning of this woman's, or of anyone's automatic responses requires, as stated before, first an understanding of the problem and then the practice of the new behavior. This new behavior must be learned and must have as an aim to make it as automatic as any conditioned reflex is. It is like rerouting a river to flow along a new course, or like a train abandoning its old tracks and starting on new ones towards another destination. It is really not something so extraordinary that it cannot be accomplished. People, in their effort to adjust to life, try all along to control their impulses and develop new responses in order to reduce the conflicts between the way they had been brought up and the way they would like to be. Our process of growing up and of maturing requires constant needs of readjustment. We change. We must change if we want to live with any sense of comfort and security. It is only when we stop growing up emotionally, when we refuse to change and when we stop integrating the simmering, heterogeneous forces of the inner self and the person we have become that we remain in conflict and invite illness. When we deny the existence of conflicts we lose touch with life and with it the mastery over our own destiny as well as the recovery of our lost happiness.

Empirically, man has known all along about the precepts of changing through the practice of different attitudes to become the ideal he has set for himself. Said Plato in The Republic, "Did you ever observe how imitations beginning in early youth and continuing far in life, at length grow into habits and become a second nature affecting body, voice, and mind?"

Again, we all, in the course of life, change. We all, with the exception of the mentally disturbed, attempt to weed out obnoxious attitudes and try to replace them with more acceptable behavior. The process of assimilation undergone by various nationalities in a city like New York can serve, perhaps, as a good example for these attempts. The majority of immigrants of different cultural backgrounds and behavior attempted to replace their old attitudes with new ones towards an ideal national image, a process which actually resembles the process of reconditioning. We must admit that these changes are sometimes only surface modifications and do not necessarily affect the deeper structure of the personality. But even in the process of assimilation we can observe a change of attitude. We can see people adopting more parliamentary ways of thinking and acting, ways which may differ greatly from the ones with which they have grown up.

Religious and political conversions also may serve as examples of how a change of heart and of a different way of feeling and thinking can come about. To a lesser degree in our everyday living, most people reserve the right to "change their mind." Only foolish (immature and rigid) people hold on stubbornly to a fixed position. The more flexible, the so-called normal people, when they recognize an untenable position they have taken and discover another more sensible or desirable point of view or way of behavior, may have little difficulty to change their mind.

Signals are sharp and unmistakable signs, firmly established in the brain which communicate specific meanings or feelings to a person like fear, danger, pleasure, grief, dislike, revulsion, delight etc.

Countersignals have to be conscious, deliberately selected and precise signs which have as their purpose the uprooting of conditioned, unhealthy, or wasteful responses, and lead to new, more desirable reactions. They also must be sharp and unmistakable.

A change of signals requires an awareness of the full act of a conditioned reflex and the practice of the new response until it becomes a new conditioned response.

We may say that the recognition of signals are diagnostic signs, while the countersignals are therapeutic attempts to create new lines of communication in the brain toward responses of our own creation and goals of our own will— with the grand aim of achieving a life of happiness.

10.

If You Can't CURE Your Neurosis—Use It

EACH NEUROSIS IS AS UNIQUE AS THE INDIVIDUAL PERSONAL-
ITY that harbors it. While each case may differ from another
in the expression and degree of the feelings of anxiety, guilt,
frustration, hostility, persecution, inferiority, or depression,
they all have a similar origin in a weak ego, if we use a
Freudian term, or too strong a degree of inhibition, if we
use a Pavlovian term.

Whether over-inhibition or too weak an ego—I prefer
using the latter term—when the patient cannot resolve the
conflict between his pressing instinctual needs on the one
hand, and his over-control on the other—he must, if he does
not want to die, change his attitude toward reality. Escaping it won't help because an obsessive compulsive neurosis causes tensions which like bottled energy, keep on exerting their pressure. And because such pressure is relentless
in its aim to seek release, regardless of its basic nature—be it
fear, guilt, insecurity, anger, a sense of persecution, or depression—it is unhealthy. It limits the balanced functioning
of the individual, and it causes suffering. The drive itself
can be outright destructive or it can, if it seeks a compensa-
tory expression, lead to creation.

One person with a neurotic feeling of inferiority may
become withdrawn, inhibited, and bitter, while another
may compensate for his feelings of inferiority by brash,
boastful aggressiveness intended to cover up his impedi-
ment by proving the opposite, that he is not inferior to
others as he feels, but superior. But regardless of how well
he may succeed, chances are that he remains unhappy,
because he still has his neurotic responses to stimuli or set
signals, which does not give him peace. If we assume that
this could be removed without a real adjustment, he may be

149

left without any drive at all, which in a competitive society may make him feel worse off than before. He then would become apathetic and lose interest in life and its accomplishments.

Many people equate creativity in its purest form with the productive power of the creative artist, and this in turn is assumed to be due to the power of his neurotic drive. This is not quite true because the scientist in his laboratory, the engineer behind his drafting table, and the cook who concocts a new dish may feel equally compelled to create, though perhaps in a less spectacular form and as the result of a lesser expression of his neurosis. However, many artists think that without their neurotic drive their work would become "flat," meaningless, or insignificant. And because artists frequently recognize the productive power of their neurotic drive, they would rather live through tortures than have their neurosis treated for fear that a cure may mean a dissipation of their talent.

A young actress who had come to see me expressed intense anxiety about this point, although as an individual she suffered severe depressions and as an artist she was unsuccessful. She was a passive, almost withdrawn personality, yet she nursed a relentless and persistent desire to achieve a spectacular success on the stage. As we have stated, severely inhibited personalities compensate for their poor self-image by setting for themselves extraordinary standards, which frequently conflict with their talent or their ability to organize their lives. They disdain an average life of average success, and must strive for an exalted place in the sun to convince themselves and everybody else of their worth. Often they are aware of how unreasonable their ambitious dreams might seem to an objective observer, and they prefer to keep the secret to themselves while they enjoy or are being kept alive by the fantasy that one day they will astonish the world, which will then pay tribute to them and regret that it had treated them so shabbily. Some of these personalities publicly proclaim lofty objectives in order to persuade others of their superiority, although any such achievement is extremely unlikely. However, when in time, one castle in the air after another tumbles down and the fantasy splinters in a clash with reality, such a person cannot help but feel overcome by failure and, most of the time, react with only greater self-rejection and deeper fits of depression.

The case of the young actress, although she was obviously talented, was nevertheless difficult for many reasons. Her dreams of stardom were not unusual among people in the theatrical profession. It might almost be said that without the narcissism and exhibitionism that go with it, no one could endure the disappointments, indignities, rejections, and delays of a theatrical career, especially in a place like New York City.

The young actress expressed admiration for her mother and a complete lack of any genuine feeling for her father. She actually felt contempt for his weakness. Yet further examination showed that while she outwardly had adapted her mother's subtle rejection of her father she was nevertheless dependent upon him. His personality demanded such dependency and, yet, she could not help but challenge his authority.

She defeated herself. She was not aware that she allowed casting directors to affect her in the same way her father did, which caused her to fear and resent them even before she had a chance to display her talent. What she feared was the very dependence she sought. What she resented was what she called male arrogance in a position of power. She was actually blocked not so much by a casting director, who, most of the time, was a total stranger to her, but by her own fears and dependency needs. By her hostile cover-up and resistance she was of course acting against her own best interests and defeating her purposes.

She was aware of her neurosis. She also realized that without the bottled tensions which kept driving her into new efforts she would never be able to make a name for herself, and so she feared psychotherapeutic treatment even more than she feared her own inhibition or the ultimate verdict of failure. However, having struggled a few years by herself—not too successfully, we may add—she did return for treatments. She worked hard on herself and learned self-control and a cultivation of her talent. She did become a star on Broadway.

The uncontrolled neurotic person is often called 'temperamental' and may not always be pleasant company. He cannot relax. His tensions can be felt; his restless drive is insatiable. When such a restlessness takes the form of a controlled drive for perfection and is coupled with talent, it creates a great artist.

A story is told that when Napoleon brought his mother to

151

Paris after his coronation as emperor of France he proudly showed her the splendid palace in which he lived. This was a moment of triumph for him, and deeply hidden under his determination was a boy who wished to make his mother happy. Did he know that the incentive for his relentless drive for more glory was a desire to please his mother or the image he had of her and to prove to her that he was worthy of her love? Hungrily he awaited a word of acceptance from his mother.

Did she praise him? The classic answer she gave expressed her lack of genuine belief in her son: "If it would only last!"

Did anyone realize the weight of this fateful remark? Did his mother know its deeper meaning? Did Napoleon feel the pain of her doubt? Perhaps, had she then been able to bestow upon her son the approval he craved, he might have experienced the happiness of acceptance; he might have relaxed, and perhaps the course of history might have been changed. But the mother could not help being the person she was, and Napoleon reacted as he had in the past. He had to keep driving on to follow the blind, powerful incentive to prove to her his worthiness, well covered-up and rationalized as the creating of a new and more liberal world. The determined boy in the man had to show that the conquest of a reactionary and decrepit world would dispel her doubts that his empire would, indeed, last.

I had a similar though considerably more modest situation with one of my patients. "I doubt if I can cure your neurosis," I had occasion to say to him, "but you suffer not so much from your neurosis as you do from the intense frustration of failure to attain your neurotic goal." The drive to perfection was, in this case, motivated by a need to impress his mother. The mother remained unimpressed.

The patient, who had become a leading fashion photographer, suffered not because of his neurotic drive to please his mother, a drive which had actually propelled him to prominence, but from his mother's rejection when she summoned up her opinion of her son's work by saying, "I don't understand how Americans can be so foolish as to pay so much money for a picture which I remember could be had in my home town in Italy for only five lire." This patient's neurotic drive and artistic temperament had provided him with a reputation and the comforts of living. But all this left him unsatisfied. Unknowingly he continued to long for his mother's praise, which she, equally unknowingly continued to withhold, because by the time my patient was born, she was thoroughly hating her husband and his creation, the son.

My patient was the younger of two sons. Somewhere in his infancy or early in childhood he became convinced that his mother's favorite was the older brother.

Creative artists, besides feeling meaningless and unacceptable as people without the passport of their creative expression often say that without the drive of their neurosis they fear a lack of incentive—and are troubled by the anxiety that their work would not have the daring colors, or the brilliance, or the force which their neurosis gives them. Because of this fear, many artists like the young actress, continue to live a tortured existence hoping that the achievement of some great success will finally deliver them from their torment and give them the acceptance they so intensely crave. Finally winning acceptance will bring them—they believe—the happiness and, like in the fairytale, all will be well.

While it is true that fame can help to diminish a person's deep sense of inferiority, and that a neurotic drive can indeed be a powerful incentive to impel a person to create, fame is not a cure-all for ill health or unhappiness while by the same token emotional health does not at all mean the end of an individual's creativity. On the contrary, sometimes the recognition of the morbid features in the neurosis of an artist may lead to an elimination of destructive inhibition and distortion and detouring, and thereby become a first step toward an integration and channeling of his purely creative drives. It is, of course, also possible that psychoanalysis may prove to a patient that his artistic genius was pure fantasy, without any basis in reality, and that he could be successful in areas other than the arts.

Laboratory experiments and life experiences have demonstrated that a first conditioning can be so strong that it will obstinately resist attempts at changing it. It provides for such individuals a sense of security and a promise of survival. They reason that even if the going may be rough they have managed in the past and hope to overcome present obstacles as well, while a change of personality by reconditioning might leave them vulnerable to other unknown dangers.

If the neurotic adaptation of a first conditioning has allowed a person to achieve some success or a promise of success, he may resist any attempt to cure his neurosis. And, indeed, some people have made a successful though neurotic adaptation to life and rightly feel that a change would shake their very existence. But this kind of person will not readily seek help. Such people want to have their symptoms treated when symptoms appear, but not the source of their neurosis. Their compulsions may have carried them far. Their psychosomatic illness may have proved to be a very convenient shield. Their drive to power may have satisfied their neurotic ambitions, and may have earned them respect and money. They may not be happy people but they have gained some fulfillment by living out their neurotic needs.

Our consideration, then, is to ask ourselves how disturbed we are, or how unhappy, or how ill, or what it is that is causing us pain. Beyond these questions, a doctor will ask if a patient is a threat to himself or to society, and whether treatment will benefit him or not.

The attempted cure of neurosis can indeed cause an individual to give up his belief in his mission and leave him without a reason for his existence. He then may have to face the full truth of his inadequacy, his maimed image of himself, or he may find himself totally alienated from himself, or find others believing that he is beyond repair. Indeed, an overambitious doctor may even cause such a patient to crack up. True, such a patient may have had a psychotic personality structure and may have just been able to get by. But exposure to his dreaded fear of facing an unacceptable reality may produce a deep and prolonged state of protective inhibition and a break with reality.

A treatment, in the words of Freud, ". . . must be profitable and not harmful." We must not forget that a neurosis has developed, after all, as a protective structure, and was meant to shield a young, weak ego in its struggle with a confusing, hostile world.

What is important for us to understand is that psychic energy can undergo a process of alteration, modification, and conversion, and that in our everyday lives we are often totally unaware of either the original drive or the forces and motivations which have produced an action or an attitude.

Many people who feel frustrated and unable to get rid of their hostile feelings or their painful inhibitions have learned to release their bottled energy in some other way. An angry woman may compulsively clean her kitchen, an executive may swing his golf club with extra force. One man may go to a gym for a workout while another may seek out some manual work or a walk of several miles. All such activities are aggressive acts that absorb arousing fighting energy and, like the steam escaping from the safety valve of an engine, safeguard the individual. These actions do not resolve the problem but they give us pause to think. The more mature person will do all these things but then try to understand the origin of the neurosis, and how it has become a conditioned response. He will attempt to sublimate these powerful energies by reconditioning and then channel them into productive or pleasurable pursuits.

A drive close to a degree of madness is necessary to overcome all obstacles in order to reach an exalted objective, and to resist the many temptations and distractions of the normal enjoyment of life. Most of man's greatest achievements, whether in art, science, politics or teaching, have been produced by men who possessed a streak of madness which drove them on, and enabled them to reject defeat and failure and to give up many pleasures and comforts they could have settled for. In the light of today's understanding we call this relentless drive to some distant goal "neurotic."

Whether a man turns his imagination to the field of creative thought or creative art depends, according to Pavlov, on his early conditioning. In addition to his four personality types, Pavlov also divided people into two groups, artists and thinkers, the former depending chiefly upon the primary (or emotional) set of signals, and the latter the second signaling systems. Poets, writers, doctors, scientists, engineers, and businessmen have made outstanding contributions when their work was compelled by their neurotic drive, which they had learned to use and to channel toward a meaningful goal.

In a less spectacular way, a conscientious artisan, a skilled worker, a housewife, can equally find a pleasurable release of his or her neurotic drive by doing what they do with devotion and intensity rather than treating their work as a chore, thereby making it creative.

All men, even the dependent and inhibited, have aggressive drives as part of their physical and psychic constitution. These are powerful forces which must seek release and which, to satisfy our own standards and those set by society, must have a meaning. The aggressive drives, when they are not released, but held back, create tensions within us, while the discharge of these aggressive drives is pleasurable because it releases the tensions.

There are in each generation only a handful of men who follow their destiny and move toward their goal undeterred—and as far as their physical and psychic energy allows them to go. They, like many scientists, don't think in terms of honors, positions or awards. They do what they feel they have to do by following their inner natural need of fulfillment. Some of this utter naturalness struck me when with some awe I was observing Albert Einstein at a time he stayed with me as a guest for several days. The average man, in a high or low position, also follows his path determined by a vast complexity of inner or outer conditioning and circumstances.

Many a man may discover sooner or later that he is no longer on the road he has chosen for his life. It is often the case that pursuit of the means to an end becomes so enjoyable, and the awareness of one's growing abilities and strength so pleasurable that the end itself becomes lost to view. By pursuing little, immediate goals we may have lost sight of the greater ones which we hoped would earn us the love, admiration, and approval that to a greater or lesser degree most people so desperately desire. Such a person is a player to whom the game has become more important than the score. In the excitement, with the crowd applauding he forgets himself. But because all the activity is actually only a means toward an end, at some point, when the game begins to be boring or when it may not demand all of the player's energies, we may find him becoming bored, disillusioned, frightened, tense, frustrated, or depressed, with a lessening of interest in the daily pursuit of business, of living, and of happiness.

There are many ways of releasing aggressive drives. Essentially these drives are dynamic energy, and any expenditure of energy in a continuous interplay of excitation and inhibition perpetually aimed at achieving a state of balance is a cycle that repeats itself endlessly throughout the course of our lives. Intense physical exercise or joyful emotional excitement serves as a swift release of energy and is pleasurable. If a person's aggressive drive is harnessed and released with a purpose, it can be used for constructive living. Channeled toward an objective such a drive can serve to make successful artists, bankers, salesmen, but even though they may become successful, they are not necessarily happy people. In fact, many are often unhappy because happiness is the end result of something else.

Happiness, in such cases, is believed to be the satisfaction of the existing neurotic needs, but because they are neurotic, they are short-lived, and because of their neurotic nature they are forever making new demands. The reason why many people are unhappy is that they have been motivated by the mistaken belief that happiness will come to them once they have reached their professional goal, a position of stardom or power or prestige, or when they would build their first home or would make their first million dollars or when they could send their children to college or save enough money for their old age—and when they then realize that all these accomplishments are the result of outer conventional needs but that as human beings they have failed to grow, that as people they have not been able to really share with another human being basic, genuine feelings such as love, sex, work, play or an hour of leisure.

Unhappy people in order to enjoy their existence must, therefore, gain an understanding of what their neurotic needs are. Satisfaction can come either by learning to live with these needs or by learning to get rid of them. The neurosis is a craving, a constant hunger, mostly unconscious and without relation to reality.

A neurosis is a conflict between man's animalistic needs and his civilized social order, between his desire and reality. There is hardly any individual touched by civilization who is not neurotic. If Diogenes were to return now with his lantern, he probably would find it easier to locate an honest man than a man without neurosis. Our problem is to learn how we can live with our neurosis and how well or how poorly we can sublimate this raw energy.

Being in conflict with reality and having undergone a process of civilization for thousands of generations, man has lost a great deal of the conscious awareness of many of his desires, especially those which are strictly repressed because they are forbidden. But these desires can and do exert a pressure through many converted symptoms, although we may not be wholly conscious of them, or they may not be

157

fully realized, or we may not always be able to express them in words. To some extent we still sense the existence of our deeper needs, and in our dreams we have the bluntness of savages who unhesitatingly express these needs.

When reality does not accord with desire, it creates conflicts which make us nervous. Our desire may be for love, sex, play, companionship, and therefore our attentions may be elsewhere when reality calls us to work. Or we may realize that we have to cultivate these needs because of single-mindedness of purpose. We may go on wanting protection, safety, comfort, or we may wish to flee a disturbing situation while our pride, guilt, fear, hunger, or training will not allow us to retreat. Then such conflict can make us tense and unhappy.

A familiar figure, often a comic one in movies, plays, and novels, is the unhappy rich man. He has so much money he lights his cigars with ten-dollar bills, which disturbs many a frustrated obsessive onlooker who is poor. He lives in luxury. He is the head of a giant corporation, where his power is absolute. Everyone trembles in his presence. Presumably he may have whatever he wants whenever he wants it. Yet, he is shown to be short-tempered, disliked, and profoundly unhappy, suffering from ulcers or worse, and living on rigid diets and baby foods. Often the reason given for his unhappiness is that he is overworked or unloved. The reason such a character is believed at all is that he bears a resemblance to an original in real life. There are such people, and we have known or read about them.

"Humor," Freud said, "is a triumph not only of the ego, but also of the pleasure principle . . ." As children we screamed with joy when our teacher stumbled. His absolutism broken, though only momentarily, reconciled us with our smallness. Therefore, we found it hilarious. Therefore, the millionaire in trouble strikes us as funny.

Also, we gloat when this tragic figure, who can be made to look so comical on the stage, is unhappy because his inner tensions, the nature of which he does not know, give him no rest. We may even reconcile ourselves to our less fortunate fate and say that at least we have our health. With little sympathy we relax by watching the poor rich man drive himself. We wonder why he does so and speculate that the acquisition of power has not done him much good, because he is still vulnerable and inhibited, still sensitive to rejection. As wise onlookers we may say to ourselves that he would not have to do all that driving, proving, and pushing, while remaining dissatisfied or making himself ill, if he could understand the neurotic motivation for all this, and if he could come to like himself and, consequently, learn to like others instead of grabbing what he wants.

Among my patients, although they are not all rich—indeed, many struggle hard to be able to afford treatment—and although some are simple people who do not suffer from peptic ulcers, there are some who fit the description of the poor rich man. One in particular I remember. He was a man in his late fifties. Besides being the head of a huge international corporation and possessing great wealth, all of his own making, he had many cultural and artistic interests which should have been a source of satisfaction to him for many reasons, not the least of them being that he began his career in extreme poverty. In his teens he had to assume support of a large family because of the death of his father. He knew the meaning of hard physical labor. He knew weariness, hunger, and humiliation, and he also knew how hard it was to lift oneself from the lowest economic level. He formed an abiding hatred of poverty which was an incentive to driving him on. Though he now has more wealth and power than he needs, and could not in his lifetime possibly spend all his money in luxurious living, he is still fighting poverty so intensely that he cannot allow himself the pleasure of a single meal without some important long-distance telephone call to interrupt him or some project on his mind that makes his tensions felt by everyone who comes near him. Even his wife is no exception. No matter how hard she has tried to adjust herself to his mercurial temperament, she has felt more and more isolated from him, which has made it increasingly difficult to live with him.

A man who has lived at a certain neurotic pace for a long period of time may not want to cure his neurosis because he cannot really think of any other way of life. He may feel driven without rest, but he may prefer this to a bland, empty existence. Such a man has lived with his neurotic compulsion for so long that a removal of it would threaten his very existence. If the patient in this case should have to give up his fight against poverty, he would be in danger of losing all interest in life. He has become conditioned to his obsessive-compulsive character structure and, therefore, could not stop. Yet, his tensions are wearing him out, and his anxiety is spoiling his life and that of everyone associated with him, making him a miserably unhappy man.

Anyone who can learn to accept the fact that he is unhappy because he dares not give of himself for fear of being hurt, or because he tries to satisfy childish and unnecessary needs, can also learn to break through his emotional isolationism. He can allow himself the freedom to feel and to relate to another human being. By the process of conditioning he can learn to practice emotional generosity and channel his energies toward more meaningful goals. He can acquire the art of becoming a happy person.

In the case of this patient, he understood that fighting poverty as a present threat to himself was quite irrational, except that he had learned to enjoy the excitement of the fight. He learned that to fight poverty as a threat to others meant an added challenge to him, gave his life extra zest. There have been many others like him who turned to philanthropy as a sincere motivation when their personal wants were secure, although the analyst might say that they were motivated by guilt or vanity.

To cure a neurosis is no easy undertaking. After all, to the neurotic his responses are normal and they are automatic reflex actions. But besides this, there are situations when a cure, even if possible, would not be advisable or would even be dangerous. Consider a politician whose intense neurotic drive has made him an orator, crusader, lawmaker, and concerned citizen of the world. The achievement of his objectives gives him great satisfaction, which to him outweighs the deprivations and the hard labor it cost him. If his neurosis is taken from him, if the illusion of his contribution goes, he is most likely to become a mediocre, unproductive, miserable, or even unhealthy individual. A driving incentive, then, would be halted, and high and weighty principles would give way to little problems of survival. With a hampered release of aggressive energy and with the ideals taken from him, he would, besides becoming less prolific, also become depressed and unhappy.

Unless such a person can create another, more meaningful goal, like heading an eminent enterprise, he would function better with his neurosis, although an understanding of his motivating drives would make him more efficient, would eliminate unnecessary anxiety, and would provide a saving in physical and psychic energy.

In brief, there are individuals who are better off not having their neuroses cured, but learning to understand the nature of their disturbed psycho-dynamic functioning, so that they can avoid dissipation and the pursuit of useless goals, and pour their neurotic drives into meaningful channels toward gratifying objectives.

Dealing with neuroses, the criterion, then, is to determine how happy or unhappy the individual is and how tolerable or intolerable his tensions are.

Chronic unhappiness is an illness that needs attention as urgently as any of the physical disturbances, like hypertension, peptic ulcer, rheumatoid arthritis, and other illnesses, the causes of which we begin to recognize as psychosomatic. How can we help ourselves?

The recognition of our type of personality can greatly help us to determine a course of action. The needs, the scope of a goal, and even the method will differ according to whether we are an adjusted, a hostile-aggressive, a dependent, or a withdrawn person, for each of us will move at a certain pace, and toward or away from life. One person will seek an area of creation. Another will be primarily motivated by his need for protection, while the withdrawn type will want evasion and non-participation. Each type will suffer conflict when he has to perform in a manner that opposes his conditioning. The outgoing, aggressive type cannot stand isolation, and the withdrawn type suffers intense anxiety when he has to be in the limelight and act aggressively.

The neurotic individual who desires to ease his tensions needs to discover the type of inhibition that interferes with his normal responses of excitation, which is action. Are his inhibitions caused by fear, guilt, unfulfilled dependency, anxiety, sexual frustration, unreleased hostility, self-doubt, insecurity, or some other type of conflict?

Indecision and procrastination are behavioral traits of the neurotic. Therefore, we must discover the "Gordian Knot," which ties us to inactivity or procrastination. What are the signals to which we react neurotically? What counter-signals can we set up for ourselves?

The answer to these questions—and, of course, there are others—can help us to determine whether a change of personality designed to cure our neurosis is desirable or at all possible, and what must be done to restore a state of balanced—that is natural—functioning of the forces of excitation and inhibition. In some respects each individual deals with and often uses his neurosis in his attempts to adapt to life. The hostile-aggressive personality, the compulsive doer, needs to build his house near a rumbling Vesuvius and seeks out danger as a greater incentive for the release of his otherwise unbearable tensions or to prove himself strong and capable enough to undertake an always greater task.

The adjusted personality achieves his balanced condition by the continuous application of healthy self-criticism, and by balancing his aggressive drives with the inhibiting rules of an organized society, yet never losing sight of the meaningful goal toward which he aims. Since life is always changing, his standards have to be examined, reviewed, and readjusted all the time. The process becomes a natural way of functioning.

The passive-dependent personality is in conflict if he denies his basic needs of dependency. Or, worse, if he pretends to be independent while he is actually living in a state of dependency, or if he enjoys such a state and denies it to himself. If he does not try to attain complete independence and if he accepts his need of some authoritative protection, he can find happiness in such a human relationship. Many intellectual, productive men and distinguished statesmen have lived contentedly in such a relationship, and have poured their independence of thought, drive, and intellectual capacity into their work.

The withdrawn individual, unless he is a psychotically sick personality, uses his neurotic need for isolation by selecting his work or profession accordingly. We may find such a person in the seclusion of a laboratory, or a library, or behind the ticket counter of a subway, or any quiet place where he does not have to deal with other people too actively.

We have stressed the point that it is not easy to gain self-understanding and to be honest with oneself. Our mental defenses get in the way. But honesty is a prerequisite to understanding ourselves and others, just as understanding ourselves and others makes it easier and more possible to be honest. If a captain of industry, whose merest gesture makes

162

thousands shudder, hungers for a crumb of praise from the people he dominates, he may do well to recognize that what he seeks is praise and that power is a means toward that objective. Understanding this will help him try to find it in a more suitable place or to question why he still needs it. By adaptation he then has a chance of becoming a happier person. By the same token, if other people recognize the nature of their fear of him, it makes them happier, too. Removal of all our neurotic drives, without proper substitution, even if it were at all possible, would leave us with a void, without incentives other than the fulfillment of basic physical needs.

Perhaps the greatest difficulty in anyone's life is to make the transition from the unconscious need to please a mother, father, or some other image, to the conscious consideration of oneself as being worthy enough to strive for and attain a set goal for himself. A goal that must however be in harmony with one's own set of standards, and avoid guilt by not violating the rights of others. As we go on practicing the art of living, we may review and revise our standards. We may give up obstructionism but also stop being our own slave driver. We may then find that there is no need to punish ourselves, to indulge ourselves, or to be discontented with ourselves if we have not fulfilled a rigid daily schedule. We can afford to relax without guilt and to be a bit kinder with ourselves. We can learn to live more contentedly with our neurotic makeup, or even make use of this source of driving energy rather than allow it to whip us to exhaustion, and drain us of our energy for work and play and companionship. But clarity and understanding are the necessary first steps if we want to appraise ourselves and our neurosis. In order to achieve this goal we must want it, and we must be resolutely honest with ourselves.

11.

RE-EVALUATION of Values

IT IS NATURAL AND, FROM A POINT OF MENTAL HEALTH, actually desirable for parents and children to disagree, for otherwise we would not outgrow our docile, childish dependency and the world would remain forever in a state of stagnation. The battle between parents and children is healthy so long as the parents realize that their children's struggle for independence is natural and so long as this struggle does not deteriorate into a destructive war of attrition in which the parents attempt to maintain their control while the children striving for independence continue to resent their dependency.

But when a set of values is forced on a child like a suit of armor, squashing his emotional growth, and when a parent is not able to build a bridge of understanding to the inner life of the child, we have an irreconcilable conflict which leads, if not to tragedy, to a great deal of alienation, pain and unhappiness. Offsprings who cannot accept the values of their parents must either break with them or, since no human can remain in a state of suspended animation, regress and die before they can blossom.

What then, may we ask, is a good child-parent relationship? Must it be as the great American lawyer, Clarence Darrow, who spent his life defending the underdog, put it, that "the first part of our lives is ruined by our parents and the second part by our children"? Where does one turn for guidance? If disciplined, Spartan upbringing is harmful, is the opposite—permissiveness and acquiescence—necessarily better? As is so often the case, the answer lies with neither extreme. Neither philosophical nor religious doctrines, but nature itself demands that the child be prepared for life without the use of force or fear. But then, as soon as the maturing specimen, whatever the species, can take care of itself it should be on its own, except that in our highly structured civilization the long years of learning delay an early break and bring about a longer time of precarious coexistence.

The child needs discipline and actually wants it, but discipline must not be confused with a rigid over-control or with a strangling of the child's need for self-expression. We have presented many examples of unhappy child-parent relationships, and we may sometimes wonder if there is such a thing as a good and healthy state of coexistence? Of course, there is, just as there is such a thing as a happy marriage.

However, it must be said that I am at a point of disadvantage here, for people who, as someone put it, have had the wisdom to select wise and understanding parents, and have therefore had a truly happy childhood, do not make up the majority of patients in my office and, probably, not in other doctors' offices. While every child will naturally struggle against the disciplining of his instinctual drives, he is never really unhappy because of it. The child wants to learn, and he accepts discipline if it is consistent, if it is free from threats and anger, if it does not crush his self-respect, and if it is rewarding because it earns him his parents' approval while leaving him enough room for exploring and developing his own personality.

The question to be answered is, do the method and principles which are being applied respect the needs of the child and his dignity, and is the love that is being given unconditional, non-judgmental, and unpossessive?

No one who deals with human problems and human tragedies can help but appreciate the deep devotion many of the people who come for help feel for their parents. Even if these grown-up children say they hate and resent one or both parents, underneath they want to love and respect their parents or at least have some understanding or workable relationship with them. They gratefully remember acts of kindness, concern, and sacrifice. Even if a child fought hard against the mother or attacked the father, once he has gained independence, he tends to remember more warmly their love than their punishments.

Years ago I was surprised when a thirteen-year-old girl, whose mother had made an appointment for her, said simply that she wanted to be my patient. Intercepting my appraisal, this anxious and serious-looking girl who tried hard to appear grown-up said determinedly, "Do you think I'm too young to have problems?" And she went on to explain that she had no one to talk to, but had once opened her heart to her older sister, who had consulted me a few years earlier. It was then that she decided to tell her parents that this, a consultation with me, was what she wanted as a Christmas gift.

The parents could not have been more astonished by this request, for the girl—let us call her Linda—was an apparently outgoing and well-adjusted child. They had no awareness of their daughter's feelings of confusion and unhappiness.

Linda was tall for her age and very pretty except for gold braces which she wore to straighten her teeth. She had been a good student until a year ago and, although she was popular, she did not really feel close to anyone.

Adolescents have problems because of their bodily growth, because of their sexual awakening, and because of their social adjustment. On the one hand, they are told that they are not children anymore, and on the other, they are warned that they are not yet adults.

Linda burst forth with her problem, which she said was her father. "I just don't like him," she said and explained that he had a peculiar talent for saying the wrong thing, and which was calculated to embarrass her most. For instance, "If I have no date for the weekend, he will tactlessly ask me what I am going to be doing that weekend. He just has a way of making me feel terrible and humiliated." She thought that most of her problems would be gone if he would only leave her alone.

After this first visit, I had a meeting with Linda's parents, who seemed understanding enough about the problems of an adolescent. The father, who thought he was affectionate as he pictured a concerned and loving parent to be, shook his head in some bewilderment. Nevertheless, he promised to leave his daughter alone. "I love her," he said, "but I won't pay any attention to her."

I did not see the girl again for about half a year, until she returned because of a new problem which had developed. She had suddenly become aware that her problem was not her father, who had indeed left her alone and with whom therefore she got along much better, but her mother. Linda had skipped a grade in school and, although the school work was not difficult, she started getting poor marks. This seemed to upset the mother, who insisted on knowing what had happened. The girl complained that her mother was overambitious and thereby destroyed her pleasure in doing well in school. There were arguments during which the girl said that she did not want to be as efficient, as ambitious, as secure and as confident as mother.

In her desire not to be like mother she had decided to be different; that is, the opposite of what mother expected. She became angry and defiant about mother's constant demand that she behave like a lady, or be more mature, or less moody, or more outgoing, or to tell her mother all her secrets or what bothered her. In her desperate need to be herself, the girl became obstructive and her school work suffered. She became resentful about mother's curiosity and her solicitude in wanting to know everything about what the girl thought, felt, or planned, and how things were going in school. In the past she and her mother had been quite chummy, but now, feeling that she was growing up, Linda began to resent mother's invasion of her private life.

Linda had problems. She was troubled by doubts about what kind of person she really was, whether she loved or resented her mother, whether she was fully honest or too selfish, or whether she had any genuine feeling for anyone. She was annoyed with herself for feeling tense with a boy, and she felt embarrassed about not knowing what to say when she was with people she respected.

Linda was not aware that she liked her father much more than she would dare to admit to herself and that her resentment of him was a defense against her awakening, unconscious sexual feelings for him, feelings stirred by her, as yet, unresolved Oedipus complex.

The problems this girl had were not really any different from those of most adolescents who struggle for their independence. Often parents may be unaware of this need or may even be amused by their children's awkward attempts to appear grown-up. It must be said to the credit of Linda's parents that they realized the problems their daughter was having and, although they felt the need to be helpful and felt sympathetic for the girl's struggles, they resisted the temptation to interfere, and they allowed their daughter enough freedom to work out her own problems.

Linda was much more conventional than she realized, and in her inexperience and uncertainty she felt restricted and unhappy. But having a chance to vent her many resentments and criticisms, and feeling quite important in discussing them with a doctor, she could relax and adjust more readily to the customs and demands of her home. No further treatment was necessary at that time.

Six years later, however, Linda came back. She was in college now, and she insisted that her parents should not know about this visit. Her problem was a conflict she had about two different boys, and the pressure of indecision disturbed her greatly. Both boys were students. One fulfilled her ambitions and standards, but it was the other boy who, she felt, was the warmer personality. She felt more comfortable with him and actually liked him better. Instead of making herself more unhappy than she already was, she thought she would talk the problem over with me.

A few weeks later she telephoned to tell me that she had made her decision and that a second visit was not necessary because all was going well. She had decided on the second boy, although his family background was a modest one which would not impress her mother or her girl friends and would probably injure her mother's ambitious social standards.

This case was uncomplicated because the parents showed understanding and respect for their growing child, and left her alone to find herself. Therefore, there existed a minimum of rebellion and frustration, which helped this adolescent in making a mature adjustment to her parents and to life. And because she basically trusted her parents, Linda could enter a trusting relationship with other people, including the boy she wanted to marry. The point of advantage Linda had was that she had been given the freedom to develop her independence away from submissive conformity and toward responsible adjustment.

In their struggle for an identity, children veer along a narrow path walled by what is permissible or forbidden and by what is commendable or ridiculous. Testing the reality of the kaleidoscopic situations around them, they learn by trial and error what they can get away with and what they cannot. The adolescent has not always learned, as yet, to curb the acting-out of the wishful thinking of the younger child, which, in the words of Freud, "is like the primitive thinking of a savage, and both are similar to the thought processes of the psychotic."

Training, as well as his comparative weakness, stops the young child from improper uninhibited behavior, but he tries, nevertheless. He shows his discontent and rage. He tries to assert himself and to make thine mine, only to find out that that gets him into trouble. If he takes his brother's toy he is scolded for it, and then, in order to soothe his pride, learns to rationalize by telling himself that he doesn't want it anyway, like the fox in Aesop's fable who could not have the grapes he wanted and used the defense of rationalizing to convince himself that they were sour.

But the child's anger may be greater, and he may break the toy or hide it away. If this is discovered, he is in trouble again and he is punished. To live by the law is, indeed, difficult. If, for instance, he borrows his friend's tricycle, he is accused of "stealing." If he soils his pants he is told he is a "pig." If, out of natural curiosity, he compares his anatomy with that of an equally inquisitive little girl, who then tells her mother, he learns that he is "wicked." If he masturbates, he is admonished as "a bad boy." If he loses a fight, he is called a "sissy." If he wins, he is a "bully." And if he obediently avoids rough games, he is called a "cream puff."

Whatever his natural curiosity prompts him to do, he runs the risk of being criticized, ridiculed, misunderstood, or punished. Through the admonitions of his elders he learns what is right and what is wrong, and that he must respect the values and standards of his parents, even if they don't make any sense, but which, because the parents' revered ancestors erected them, must be honored.

When he becomes an adolescent and feels his physical strength growing—while at the same time he has not gained full control over the wild, uninhibited, and sometimes frenzied rage he had when he was younger—he may feel compelled to act out his hostility, and we then have the juvenile delinquent—the confused, frustrated, angry youth whose excitation is unharnessed because it has neither direction nor purpose, except the violent and, therefore, destructive need to release his rampant energy.

It is, as a rule, the lack of love and direction such a youth has had and the brute force he experienced when he was small and defenseless that has left a sting of anger and vindictiveness in him, because he considered the treatment of the powerful adult as not being "fair." He may, later in life, behave in the same manner with his children and thereby add one more link to the long chain of unhappy conventional practice. Or he may grow up and go to the other extreme, becoming over-permissive and indulging his children.

If an open and trusting relationship between parents and children has not been cultivated in a family, it cannot be easily established later in life, and we then have what is called a generation gap. We then have a situation which reminds me of a family of porcupines who, because of the extreme cold, drew close together to keep warm but then felt the sting of their needles and pulled away until the cold made them move close together again.

I have seen the frustration of the parent-child relationship reach a tragic peak when a parent is about to die, and the grown child stands at the bedside grieved and guilt-ridden because in his anxiety he feels that he has not given the parent all the time and affection he thought the parent had a right to expect.

The parent, on the other hand, is often equally frustrated because of his inability to communicate with his sons and daughters and his inability to say good-bye, like the patriarchs in the Old Testament who, we are told, assembled their sons, and by blessing them, left them a cherished memory. The problem is that we, the living, have set up a strict taboo toward death and have shut our eyes to the meaning of death, by paraphrasing it as a "passing-away" or a "passing-on." We deprive death of its naturalness and so there is often pretense on both sides; both the dying parent, claiming to feel 'fine' while he may be suffering the pain of departing, and the child to suffer grief because of the impending loss. And so both sides deprive themselves of that intense solemn bitter-sweet emotion of love by refusing to say a natural good-bye.

When about two decades ago, I was writing my first book, *The Will to Live*, I was astonished by the scarcity of scientific material on the psychological aspects of dying patients. Stirred by the loss of my own parents within a year as well as the experience of watching many a man draw their last breath, I wrote a chapter, "Man dies when he wants to die," which a few years later led to my being invited to read a paper at a symposium on death at the American Psychological Association. Out of this symposium

170

under the capable editorship of Herman Feifel, grew a book: *The Meaning of Death*, which in turn may have stimulated a number of psychological studies on death published since then. At any rate, death being an integral part of life, rules everyone of us, consciously or unconsciously, waking or dreaming, accepting the grim fact about our end or denying it.

But while we live and struggle to maintain ourselves as well as our first conditioning allows, we move on, sometimes like somnambulists, along a course that is as charted for us as that of a satellite around a planet. We have developed mental defenses whose purpose was to protect the small, growing—and sometimes not-growing—ego of the child. These mental defenses remain in operation throughout life, and determine our behavior with other people, and the oblivion or vision of truth we have about ourselves.

The wide range of love and hate, jealousy and fear cease to be pure emotions, and become associated reflexes, for love is tempered by a fear of being hurt, and hate is tempered by a fear of being discovered and punished, jealousy is tempered by our pride and fear of ridicule, and so on.

A normally strong ego can take defeat and failure in its stride, as with a child who, while learning to walk, falls down and without any injured pride picks himself up with renewed determination. This is natural. A strong ego is not much bothered by those most immature of all emotions, pride and vanity. It re-evaluates a situation and simply makes another attempt, thereby often turning failure into success.

The weak ego cannot take defeat and it hides behind defenses. In order to protect his weak ego, the person caught red-handed in an act of foolishness or deceit may intellectualize or rationalize and say, "What else could I have done under the circumstances?" or "Perhaps the other person was not even aware of the incident" or "Perhaps it is for the best, anyhow." A bruised ego may also solve its pain, neglect, abuse, or misunderstanding by rationalizing that it is very well for the other person to believe the way he does, but "If I had his money or good looks or good fortune, I'd do even better. . ."

Whether it is exactly nine-tenths of our personality that is submerged, like the iceberg, or whether it is less, the fact is that only the smaller part is visible, not only to others, but to ourselves. We may have objectives in that nine-tenths of

171

our unconscious which could very well differ from those in the visible one-tenth of our conscious minds. Consciously, we may achieve a position of importance or glamor, or a career which will please a parent, but in the stronger, submerged part of our personality we may desire something entirely different and often veto our conscious decision. This often happens to people who try so hard to succeed but end as failures.

Another strangling mental defense mechanism is denial, a protective forgetting of emotional responses which blocks out disturbing feelings so that one can react as if they never happened, the aim being to preserve the integrity of the individual. I remember a patient who grew up in utter poverty. He tried desperately to win the affection of his mother, his stepfather, or anyone who would pay any attention to him. He remembered once, when he was on his way to school, day-dreaming as usual, that a nun waved to him. He was so overcome with joy, so filled with a feeling of what he thought was finally a sign of acceptance, that he excitedly waved back. Later, in class, the nun turned to him and in front of the class said sharply, "How dare you wave? You're a stupid boy, thinking that I would pay any attention to you. There was another nice child on the second floor I meant to greet. I would never look at a boy so poorly groomed as you are, who walks around with those big holes in his stockings."

The man never forgot the laughter of the class. "At least," he consoled himself, "the other children had fun."

There were many other similar painful experiences this patient had, like standing for hours in front of his father's store to collect his mother's five-dollar alimony, feeling terrified to come home without the money. And in order to survive all these unhappy events, his ego caused him to "deny" that they were directed against him. He compensated for the rejection, first by draining his experiences of their emotional quality, then by trying to see them in a humorous light. It is somewhat the process Charlie Chaplin and other comedians have used as a basis for their humor. The humor serves as a release from unacceptable feelings of stress and rebellion. In this case they helped the young man to become a successful writer of witty stories. But in his stories this writer was carefully avoiding the inner conflict of his characters until he learned to understand his own problems and conflicts, and the reasons why he had learned

172

to show only the non-offending, humorous situations in his stories. Realizing this and growing up emotionally, he dared to allow the characters in his stories to live more but not fully through the emotional turmoil of real people. As a result his writing improved but fell short of greatness because of his lack of allowing himself the freedom of reliving the whole, bitter reality.

The ideology with which an individual grows up has a profound influence on his development, but the character of parents and their attitudes toward human values as practiced in the home are the more determining factors in shaping the human personality. This would be discouraging if the history of human progress had not proven that man has been able each time to overcome to some degree the power of his first indoctrination and that it is within the power of the individual to accept his indoctrination or to break or to change it. It is always easier to negate the problems and to deal with tensions by making outer changes, like changing the scenery, by taking a trip, repainting a home, buying a new dress, or marrying a new wife, than to recognize the nature of our defenses and to gain the insight. Insight demands courage and hard work.

Sometimes the pent-up rebellion is so intense and the first conditioning so rigid that the person becomes inhibited to such a degree that he paralyzes the rich potentials he may possess and makes them dry up. Or sometimes there is a slow maturing and sudden eruption of a talent but not before an individual has come close to the threshold of death.

I think of the son of a friend of mine who grew up in a well-to-do home where the father tried to foster a culture that he himself had lacked in the home in which he grew up. The elderly friend had collected a fine library with many first editions, and occasionally the children were told the value of the new acquisitions. They were bored. But what was most excruciating to the son were the evenings of chamber music. Every member of the family played a different instrument, and once a week there was a concert, often with guests present. Under the stern direction of the father the boys had to display their musical talents. This particular boy had to play the cello and he dreaded the evenings, nourishing a violent hatred against the music, the instrument, and everything musical.

The war disrupted his choice of a profession. And before

173

he could finish college he found himself after D-Day on the European battlefield. There he went through one particular experience which was so terrifying that it rocked the foundation of his personality. At the battle of the bulge his division had been cut in half. Dazed by the bitter wintry cold, he stood for three days and nights glued to his anti-tank gun, frozen, hungry, numb. In his state of fear-paralysis he kept firing his gun while one after another of his comrades died and his company was reduced to a few survivors. Finally, when reinforcements came, having broken through the enemy lines, and he was safe, he collapsed. But the terror never left him.

In the army, he performed his duties as obediently as he had during his chamber music evenings, although inwardly he hated the brashness and authority in the army with the same passion that he had hated his dictatorial father and his commands. After the war he thought he should help unhappy and misunderstood children, and so he studied psychology. But his first conditioning exerted its power. Although he thought he hated music, he actually loved it, and he had learned to appreciate the beauty and emotional intensity of the works of the master composers. But he could not touch a cello. He supported himself by tuning pianos. One day, as a diversion, he built a harpsichord which, when he demonstrated it, greatly impressed the big piano manufacturers, who besieged him to join their companies. But these businessmen disturbed him. They were like his father, and he feared he would be dominated by them. He had to be on his own. Before long he began producing this rare instrument by himself. His skill and talent paid off in money and fame. And now, perhaps unaware of the deeper motivation, he returned to his family circle of music. He bought a country house, where he built a theater for musical festivals, giving young talents the chance he felt he himself never had. He was thereby living out his conditioning, and by channeling his rebellion and pouring his energies into creative pursuits he could overcome the harmful experiences of his younger life.

Every maturing human, like this young man, stops at one time of his life or another to examine the values by which he has existed and questions whether they are still valid or whether they need a reform. This is a natural process of living and maturing.

Values represent the worth of things. They relate to the esteem in which we hold ourselves, our fellow men, and the

world we live in. They also relate to our beliefs and disbe-
liefs, our religions, moral, and ethical standards, and to our
political convictions. They affect our critical sense, and they
are at the bottom of our prejudices. Values make us measure
the importance of our work and our leisure time. And values
determine the principles and ideas we form about all the
things in life we may cherish or abhor.

Because values can be an incentive as well as a hindrance
we must, in order to be able to practice the happy habit in
life, examine what values we want to cultivate and what
values we want to be rid of, including those values we have
been brought up with but later find difficult to accept.

In the process of re-evaluating our values we are obliged
to wage a running battle with our own sense of values and
those set by the society in which we live. We may feel
compelled to lower our standards, or we may dare to raise
them according to who we think we are and what we want
to be. In the search for an identity—that is, the wish to form
our own distinctive personality—we choose values which we
then strive to make an integral part of ourselves, and we do
this by practicing them.

For instance, the status seeker driven by a need of self-
importance is compelled to achieve symbols of status set up
by his group rather than by himself. The hostile-aggressive
type of person may drive himself relentlessly to ever-greater
performances without ever allowing himself the time to
relax, while the passive-dependent individual may dutiful-
ly follow his bellweather, and derive safety and minimal
pleasure from pleasing others.

Whatever road we choose, there are values to be considered. Instinct runs counter to values, and our conscience is
continuously plagued by the demands of values from within
or from without. If we recognize that some of our standards and values have outlived their usefulness, what can
we do? Do we withdraw, saying "You can't fight city hall,"
or do we fight for what we believe is right and progressive
and human against a not-caring, bureaucratic opposition?
How can values be changed anyhow?

In his essay, "Some Questions About Values," John Dewey asks himself, "Are values and valuations such that they
can be treated on a psychological basis of an allegedly
'individual' kind? Or are they so definitely and completely
socio-cultural that they can be effectively dealt with only in
that context?" In the short span of time which has elapsed

since 1944, when Dewey formulated this question, research has provided sufficient evidence to affirm the first part of his question; namely, that psychology can clarify and reconditioning can indeed treat, amend, and change values. This positive answer already weakens or makes obsolete the second part of the question: ". . . are they [the values] so definitely and completely socio-cultural that they can be effectively dealt with only in that context?" Revolution is an impatient, adolescent approach to change which appeals to the angry or violent type. It is deplored by the complacent, the passive-dependent, and repugnant to the mature. While a forceful revision of values may come about through tyrannical oppression, mature people desire change through peaceful conversion and creative progress.

Values are a product of a socio-cultural structure which is in turn continuously affected not only by religious, moral, and ethical concepts, but also by economic growth and scientific discoveries. Our lawmakers recognize the need for changes, and, although they may often lag behind their time or may act hastily, they introduce new bills to catch up with modern man's growing needs.

We consider a psychological treatment successful if it helps an individual to make a positive adjustment to his socio-cultural environment, yet allows him enough room for self-expression and, if necessary, for a reform of the values with which he grew up but cannot accept anymore. Our Western democratic way of life, in spite of many imperfections, is so far the only form of government which allows such growth. While an individual may appear to be a rebel in the eyes of the group, his search is for the truth of intrinsic values. This is how individual people have helped the progress of humanity. The driving need such a "rebel" has is less to help himself than to help his group. Whether he is a political or moral reformer, if he has reached maturity, he will choose a tolerant, democratic appraisal of human needs.

The revolutionary temperament, a hostile-aggressive type of man, cannot contain his aggression and therefore cannot wait for any gradual adjustment. He is the type that wants what he wants when he wants it, believing or deluding himself with the belief that he knows what is best for the group, often forgetting the blood he causes to be spilled.

In our era we have experienced two major and several minor revolutions that are examples of this kind of thought. Psychology rejects force and prefers the use of understanding and persuasion as tools to work with. The very nature of their profession does not allow psychologists to accept any method that violates the dignity of human beings, for the restoration of self-respect and integrity is part of their job. Dictatorial revolutionaries, on the other hand, work with threats, terror, and severe punishment, methods which caused Pavlov's dogs to break down. These inhuman means are applied by rigid or mentally ill leaders to prevent the deviation from established or newly revised values, which brings many individuals into sharp conflict with such regimes, and we have seen people go into exile in order to live with their beliefs and values. Sometimes it is not a mere matter of political persecution but of poor socio-economic conditions which have caused people to leave their homes, and seek a life of freedom and opportunity, as did the countless people who came to the United States. But whatever the motive, in the last analysis, an individual has to evaluate values and be guided by them in making his final decision.

The question of values confronts us throughout life, whether we deal with the greater issues of human rights or truth and justice. Besides lofty aims we must consider the values of beauty and of all the goals and merits that make up the fabric of a culture. Then, there are also values to be considered during special periods in our life when we feel the need of examining the worth of things, of what to accept for ourselves and what to reject. Whether this period is adolescence, or the peak of one's man- or womanhood, or the climacteric, or the time of retirement, in each case an individual has to answer for himself the question: Can I continue to exist with the values I was brought up with or by which I have lived until now? What values need reform? Understandably, the values of the septuagenarian differ from those he had a few decades earlier, if for no other reason than that he must consider the possibility of his imminent end. Therefore, regardless of how we decide, whether we are an aggressive or passive or evasive individual, in making our decision we are confronted with a reevaluation of values.

A great deal of our individual unhappiness is the result of our inability to make such a reevaluation or if we have made it, to carry it out. And, yet, we cannot ever hope to attain happiness if we don't gain clarity about the meaning of the values we wish to cherish and the civilization in which we live. It is our individual state of clarity that will enable us to distinguish between the chaff and the wheat, the values to discard and those to uphold. The many people who are confused about values can find an answer by a relentless search for the truth with regard to who they are as people and what they wish to represent.

The doctor, as a guide for many confused people, must aim to attain clarity so that he can be of help without exerting pressure or criticism. He may feel like Camus who wrote: "My role, I know is not to transform the world, nor man; for that I have not virtues enough nor clear-sightedness. But it consists, perhaps, in serving where I can those few values without which a world, even transformed, is not worth living in, without which a man, even now, could not be worthy of respect." But most of the time, values are subjective, and what we are striving for is objectivity.

12.

There is a DOOR

ONE OF MY PATIENTS OCCASIONALLY BROUGHT TO A CONSULTA-
tion little drawings which depicted her feelings. Most of the
time she appeared in them as a little girl with braids and a
big bow, wearing a small apron, looking longingly through
the iron grill of a prison at the outside.

One day her drawings showed the door of her prison
open and the arms of the little girl raised in astonishment.
Later she brought a drawing of the little girl wandering
through a garden outside her prison, smelling a big flower.
Significantly, the door of the prison remained open for a
possible quick retreat.

But one day in the picture the little girl was holding
hands with other children dancing in a circle. The door was
closed, symbolically indicating that she didn't need the
safety of her prison anymore. It is this symbol of a door
which I so often use to assure a patient who feels hopelessly
caged in that there is a way out into a world of sunshine
and, certainly, of more freedom.

Sometimes, when a patient asks what he can expect to
gain by a treatment that helps to make him understand
himself, my answer is that, if he cannot change the course of
his life, he can at least understand why he feels the way he
does and that he can overcome the claustrophobic feeling of
being trapped. Because there is a door, if he wishes to make
the effort to see it and if he chooses to walk through it.

This story, which some may remember having read in the
newspapers, is about an ex-convict who had been arrested
for burglary. He had served a long prison term for a major
robbery. Sometime after his release from prison, a sensation-
al new robbery mystified the police. The professional skill

and technique of the job made the police suspect the ex-convict. However, the burglar had carelessly left so many clues that the detectives dismissed the ex-convict as a suspect and, instead, looked for an obviously talented but inexperienced beginner. Finally, for the sake of the record, the police decided to interrogate the ex-convict, who greeted them by asking what had taken them so long to come to him. He went on to say that he hadn't known how to make it easier for them to track him down and that, because of his technique, he thought they would think of him immediately.

When the puzzled policemen asked why he wanted to go back to prison, the ex-convict said that leaving his cell had seemed to him the fulfillment of a long-awaited hope. But, now, being out had made him realize that too much time had passed and that he had become estranged from life. In prison he knew the routine. He had become adjusted to it, and the only way to go back was to commit a new crime.

This, perhaps, is the feeling many a reader may have when he comes to realize that the prison he has created for himself has a door. When he decides to stay in his prison rather than to seek freedom, his decision is a door which shuts him off from a life that seems to him too threatening, too confusing and too demanding to be desired. But the clarity of such a decision may help to eliminate the conflict between living one way of life while desiring another.

What is incompatible with a sense of ease and is so often a source of great unhappiness is the panicky feeling of restraint—of being chained down not merely by an ailing parent, a disgruntled spouse, or responsibilities toward children, but by the fear of a lively, pulsating life outside one's prison.

This was the frightening state the very confused woman was in who drew the pictures at the time when she first came to see me. Although in her thirties, she still looked like a frightened child who, with big and very sad eyes, tried to understand the dread within her and the upheaval around her. Her anxieties were at times uncontrollable. She felt entombed in a subway train or an elevator. Her careful choice of words and her precise descriptions of the disturbing situations which she experienced revealed besides her intelligence the enormous degree of her inhibitions. It was evident that in her mind she must have gone over her situation time and again only to feel more desperate and discouraged about her state of alienation.

She worked as a film editor with a television network, functioned well at her job, possessed many talents, and had a perceptive, penetrating, analytical mind. In view of all these endowments, it was pathetic to observe how after hours she fled into the safety of her lonely home.

Recent studies have confirmed a Pavlovian principle, as well as a psychological experience, that the degree of social withdrawal which is characteristic of schizophrenia depends on the degree of excitation to which the cortex of the brain and the autonomous nervous system are aroused. The greater the social withdrawal of a person, the greater his degree of arousal in the outer layers of the brain, or perhaps it is the other way around. At any rate, withdrawal cannot be called just a capricious mood, but must be considered a protective act or an illness of adaptation. The overly aroused brain cells invoke the safeguarding principle of protective inhibition. It is evident, therefore, that kindly encouragement alone cannot make these people walk out of the safety of their prison, but that they must be prepared to meet the social challenges of the outside world. This can be done by chemically calming the highly reactive cortical cells so that they respond with less excitation or by making such a person feel more secure, so that he won't view the outside world as so very dangerous, tumultuous, or frightening a place to be moving around in.

It is understandable therefore that the symbol of a door that separates two ways of life, an active one and a withdrawn one, will be looked upon differently by the different types of personalities.

The weak-inhibitory personality with the most reactive cortical cells will look at the ideal state of life as being on a faraway island or in some paradise in which there is no excitation and no struggle. This represents the Buddhist concept of utter happiness. Nirvana may theoretically mean an ideal state of existence because of its freedom from pain and passion, but it is a mental and emotional state of lifelessness and an absence of the joy of wrestling with a problem or an idea. It is therefore void of a sense of progress and accomplishment. From the viewpoint of a healthy realism, such a goal is a death-like inhibition and therefore the antithesis of life. What the weak-inhibitory individual de-

181

sires is a return to a womb-like, parasitic existence where he is cared for, where he need not make any effort or contribution, and where it is a matter of course to receive and not to give—all of which adds up to a denial of life and a gently evasive way of expressing a wish to die. At any rate it is in conflict with our Western way of life.

The hostile-aggressive personality, made unhappy by his restless inner drives, may eagerly accept the symbol of a door as a means of salvation from any restrictive existence. He aches to prove himself and his energies by pushing and racing ahead, sometimes without a clear plan to follow. And he may welcome the chance to close or slam the door of the authoritative home in which he grew up.

The passive-dependent personality may learn to give up infantile passivity, and mature by becoming less dependent and by accepting responsibilities which help to develop a greater sense of security and self-respect. To him, the knowledge of a door is a promise of a better and happier life.

The individual other than the schizophrenic, who, for reasons of neurotic safety, chooses to remain in his self-made prison, must know that the choice of such a life is his decision. He therefore cannot blame life, or the imperfection of our civilization, or some existing threat, or some other insurmountable obstacle for his unhappiness—unless, of course, his illness does not allow him such clarity of thought. No human can ever hope to attain happiness by pretending to be an adult while emotionally remaining in the immature world of the child, where, like the child, he continues to hope for a better and happier way of life without working for it. Moreover, such a person must remain in a continuous conflict because deep down his natural aggressive drives and his curiosity are bound to clash with the painful inhibitions laid down by the various taboos of the real world in which he was brought up. Many people, because they recognize the obstinacy of their conditioning and because the mere recognition of the factors which produced them does not automatically dispel the neurotic response, are pessimistic about any change in their own nature and that of the human race. We often hear people speak about the irreconcilable conflict between the beast in man and the sublimity of his spirit, and gloomily accept unhappiness to be part of the human heritage. Scientifically, such a belief is a matter of conditioning, and the morbid nature of feeling and thought is a result of developed inhibition.

Any person who has become convinced that a healthy life is controlled excitation and action, not morbid inhibition, and who has because of confusion temporarily withdrawn from life, will either pull himself out of his morass by his own bootstraps or he will seek help. Not seeking help, but remaining in a state of joyless stagnation is self-destructive. It is the mentality of the emotionally sick who often exists with some self-inflicted image of martyrdom. In such a world of darkness to recognize the tiniest amount of self-worth is necessary to make a person give up some of his passivity. If he can go on to recognize further his potentials as well as his limitations he will not be afraid to walk through a door toward a chosen goal.

But then the individual who wants to be true to himself has a variety of barriers to overcome. Besides his conditioning, which made him the passive or withdrawn type of personality, he must also cope with the tenacious power of the brainwashing to which he has been exposed and which is the sum of all that he has been taught, has read, heard, and seen, and which he unwittingly has observed by just being a product of a specific culture. No one, I dare say, except the hermit in his prison, which he may call a "haven," is completely free from what we call public opinion, which Disraeli explained as being the product of the master writers of an era. The constant bombardment to which an individual is exposed by the press, a crafty advertising industry, and radio and television tends to convert and further brainwash him until he reacts to their persuasions like the insecure, confused victim of the suggestions of a hypnotist.

But, underneath it all, the individual knows that he must take a stand and accept the responsibility for his own existence. There are people who argue that they cannot be convinced that there is any greater purpose in life and, since we all must die anyhow, see no sense in struggling on or contributing anything. To these people, life means the passing of time.

Various schools of existentialism try to give answers to the most perplexing questions of our human existence and to the seeming paradoxes around us in the universe. Religions try to console us with our fate of being small and essentially alone and of having to die.

Sometimes the doctor is asked questions which he can answer no more readily than any other human being, especially by people who wonder whether they should go on living or give up the struggle. But cognizant of the nature of his profession and his responsibility to people, the doctor, unless he himself is a withdrawn type of individual, will find reassurance enough in what he has learned and experienced, and what others have discovered before him, and it will be these facts, small as they may seem when related to the universe, that will prove strong enough to give him answers as to what to do about the preservation of a human life.

Controlled action is pleasurable. Creation secures health and has meaning. Inhibition is painful. It causes illness and danger to oneself and to other people.

Although I have said that obstacles are not a real threat to the attainment of happiness and that other eras have had their full share of problems, we seem to be experiencing a new development which imperils our individual security and is greatly threatening our pursuit of happiness. There is evidence of a growing alienation of people from one another brought about by the rapid progress of technology and the vast expansion of urban life. The ever larger communities, with their vast public services and modern conveniences, have greatly decreased the interdependence of people as it existed and still exists in rural areas.

Many people believe that they can afford to do without their neighbor and his help because the telephone allows them to call quickly for adequate help or advice or direction. They feel that they don't have to put up with moods of a neighbor or the strangers next door because the automobile and other means of communication allow them to more easily select the people they favor. Friendship, some may think, needs no cultivation anymore, because friends can be replaced quickly. The easing or downright disintegration of traditional family life, as one sees it in big cities, only furthers the process of alienation, with its not-caring attitude, pseudo-friendliness, and inner uninvolvement.

The love of the child for his parents or their substitutes is explained as being based on the child's state of helplessness and his needs. If he would not need his parents, he would often enough wish them away. The same principle, though to a lesser degree, exists in a rural area, where people need one another. They maintain warmer neighborly relationships.

The higher structure of our modern civilized life has brought with it a loss of rugged individualism and an increase in conformity, which is an inhibition of living. Inwardly alienated, modern man compensates for his self-effacement and his loss of a sense of independence by a need to belong, which makes him seek out groups, clubs, and gangs to a point where he becomes a little cog and craves for symbols in order to gain or regain a feeling of belonging and importance. It is the feeling of aloneness which Erich Fromm says causes people to give up their freedom and to submit to an authoritarian rule.

It is the alienation of man from himself and of man from man which has made possible the acts of genocide which our generation has witnessed in Hitler's gas chambers and the dropping of the atom bomb on Japan. The danger we face is not so much the accidental pushing of the fatal button triggering an all-out nuclear war, although this danger is great, but the loss of any genuinely humane feeling as a result of the inner alienation and not-caring attitude of people who are not aroused enough to resist the evolvement of a hostile genocidal movement.

Ever since the division of people between masters and serfs theoretically ended—it still goes on, as we know individually, whenever they feel trapped by dire socio-economic conditions—people have, like the nomads, sought greener pastures. They have, with little inhibition, left their unhappy surroundings. The same with their intolerable political conditions—people have walked out of their prison and gone through a door to a life of freedom where they could work, think, and act as free human beings. This is what we as individuals, once we recognize the nature of our oppressive state, can also do. There is another existence that will allow us the free release of energy toward a meaningful and enjoyable goal, and toward a life that is not imprisonment and frustration, but freedom and happiness.

13.

The Larger HAPPINESS

THE LAST CHAPTER OF A BOOK THAT HAS AS ITS THEME
man's individual struggle for happiness and as its objective
a presentation of the manifold and complex motivations of
his self-defeats, as well as how to redirect and cure them,
would be incomplete, indeed, if the author did not make an
attempt to apply the same principles he has developed
throughout the book to the world at large. After all, what
happens in the world at large is nothing but the projection
on a huge scale of forces and principles similar to those
which motivate every individual in his struggle for existence. History is not simply a sum of recorded past events
which have run their own independent course. History has
been made by individual people. As people they may have
been sane or mad, visionaries or paranoiacs, but having a
position of power, they could make fateful decisions affecting the life and culture of a society as well as the state of
war or peace, freedom or enslavement, progress or decline.
These decisions, today as in the past, are first perceived in
the minds of individual men before they are put into effect,
which means that they are subject to the way in which a
particular mind has been conditioned by the laws of aggression and inhibition, as described throughout this book.
Hence the title of this chapter, "The Larger Happiness."

During the comparatively short time that science—
following the separation of Church and State—has been in
existence and is investigating the problems of man with the
objectivity and dispassionate approach that distinguishes it
from every other method, it has already conquered many of
man's ancient plagues, the fear of diseases, and some, if not
all of his prejudices. It is science that has taught man how

to conquer hunger, to produce an abundance of food, housing, and clothing, and to make use of his world's raw materials, even if these are at present available to only a few privileged nations. And it is science's relentless offensive that is forcing nature to yield one after another of its mysteries. Man has accomplished the incredible feat of landing on the moon and in myriads of laboratories all over the world scientists labor with the problems of exploring heretofore inexplicable laws which prevail, be it in its smallest particle, the atom, or its largest, the macrocosm, so that today we see man standing awe-struck, but undeterred at the threshold of the workshop of life itself. Must we despair or doubt that science will not be able to free man from the madness of war and his long conditioning to use force as a means of settling arguments, as it has been able to cure many other means of self-destruction? Is it arrogant to believe that our century, which has seen man at his cruelest and most inhumane, should not also be able to see him at the other end of the scale, sublimating his destructive drives into truly creative pursuits worthy of the human spirit?

Freud himself, who had felt the bitter sting of prejudice, was fully aware of man's ancient problem of being victimized by the paroxysms of hate and of the denial of this hate by individuals or groups, as demonstrated by the many religious wars and crusades fought in the past in the name of love and faith. He was pessimistic about the successful application of his theories to free man as a group from the compulsiveness of inner destructive aggression. Experience has indeed justified his grim prediction, for the political storm which just one generation ago shook first Germany, then the whole world, after chasing him from his beloved Vienna, not only indulged in an unequalled orgy of blood, but burned his books and forbade the teaching of psychology. Unbridled, the forces of regression ran their abominable course with the same fury that we see in a psychotic man suddenly running amuck.

Pavlov was more optimistic. He too had to live through a bloody political revolution which he detested, but he came out of it with the hope that psychology might ultimately deliver man from his brutish conditioning and help to "perfect the human race of the future." He believed that resorting to violence and force was a conditioning that could be changed, and that war, which he described as "a bestial means of solving life's difficulties, a means unworthy of the human mind and its limitless resources," could ultimately be overcome and abolished.

Lenin's Russia at the time it won its revolution, although hungry and bled white from World War I and a long, cruel civil war, did not burn Pavlov's books but, on the contrary, built him laboratories and raised him to the status of a demigod, so that the initially defensive scientist eventually came to say that "in our country the whole population honors science," which formerly had been divorced from life and alienated from people.

Pavlov did not live to witness the disappointingly brutal rule of the government in power and the abuse of the purity of his scientific principles, applied as brainwashing, but this does not render invalid his theories or his hope. Reconditioning requires patient and concentrated efforts, and it requires scientists who won't compromise on truth and integrity to do the job, rather than rigid and bungling diplomats, who so often yield to expediency· But the desire of people for peace does not differ very much from the desire people have for health, for, as we said in the first chapter, it is not enough for a patient to go to a doctor and complain about his troubles; he must want to get well. The experience of every doctor shows that many patients just don't want to get well, whether they are conscious about it or not. And so, many people and leaders of people may speak loudly about peace but not really want it. If we again refer to Claude Bernard, the habit of complaining about being ill has turned a symptom of adaptation into a disease of adaptation. Like children who cry for help, people may cry for peace, but not until the angry child in man has grown into a mature, controlled, peace-loving being can there really be peace; otherwise, he will remain a victim of his rages and hostilities turned outward, which is war.

We have seen why the man who had started out with a good New Year's resolution failed. In a similar way we have seen the failure of individual people, groups, and nations who may have sincerely desired a life of peace without strife and hate but lapsed back into the habit of their first, restive conditioning. *Reconditioning towards peace has not failed; it just has not ever been properly applied and certainly has never been accurately practiced.*

Among the many reasons given for the cause of war, by men wiser than myself—reasons ranging from primitive prepossession of man's beastly lust for blood to the theories advocated by the master experts on socio-economic factors— none, I believe, goes really to the heart of the problem, which is to see it in the light of the elementary dynamics of excitation and inhibition. Excitation being the lustful release of aggression with the aim to annihilate threats, real or imaginary. And inhibition, the counterforce, that has grown from its original form to be protective into a paralyzing force produced by excessive fear or the demands of conditioned taboos.

There are even philosophers who subscribe to war because they see peace as a state of inhibition, which they interpret as a state of weakness, of nothingness, the end product of which is deterioration and death. War, on the other hand, they acclaim as a natural human excitation which is action, movement, bringing out courage, heroism and production, and they say it to be an incentive to invention and progress. Actually, it seems that man is much more ready to make enormous sacrifices in money and blood for war or war machines—as seen for instance in the Vietnam war, than for the exploration of the demands of a peaceful society or a peaceful world. Therefore, all that is necessary to justify the uninhibited mass murder of war is to invent an acceptable "cause" and give it a proper slogan; then we have "a good war" or "a just war" or a "necessary war" etc.

Yet, scientifically seen, the concept of equating peace with inhibition is erroneous. While war is obviously the most uninhibited form of excitation, it is so because of its total lack of control and because of the destructive methods it applies—methods similar, as I have said, to a psychotic acting out. To many war is lustful—its disguise is called defense. Even the planning of war, called "strategy," is exciting and lustful in men with a distorted, sadistic mind and to some degree paranoic way of thinking, like men who at the height of the cold war encouraged us to dig our own graves, which they euphemistically called "air raid shelters."

Peace, in order to satisfy the needs of man, must like health be a balance of the forces of excitation and inhibition. Peace therefore is not static, nor is it the mere absence of war. Peace, if it is to be attained, must aim at a full use of our aggressive drives channeled toward dynamic, sublimated, and creative goals, as the strong excitatory type we described, which showed purpose and control.

Why has man always hoped for and yet never really

189

achieved peace? Besides never having made peace an object of reconditioning, there is another problem, I believe, which becomes evident when we examine the people who are in a position of power to control the minds of their fellow men.

I think back to the first meeting of the tenants of the house in which I live, when the question of making the building a cooperative was being discussed. As the plan was presented, a few of the unquestionably hostile-aggressive type of men moved forward quickly to debate the issue. Before the more passive and deliberating people had a chance to consider the project, a few aggressive men had already formed a committee; a miniature government with a president at the top had come into existence.

The same situation exists in a community, a city, a country. The greater a politician's ability to whip up simmering hostility and discontent in people, the more cunning his ingenuity is at arousing fear of a real or trumped-up threat, the greater his chances of attaining leadership. The appeal a strong leader has for passive people lies primarily in their conditioning. Like our young lawyer in the first chapter, who was conditioned to see in every authority a powerful mother figure, passive people are patterned to follow automatically, though sometimes reluctantly, a leader who pledges to protect and to take care of them. Hitler promised to eliminate all the decadent and sick people, and to create a glorious empire of a master race served by people of inferior racial quality.

Aggressive personalities are often won over by a supple leader who represents a strong father image and whose flaming appeal promises them a fight *against* a dangerous enemy, against all that is weak and bad, and *for* all that is strong and superior, he being the supreme judge.

Aggressive people, like our disbarred lawyer, are more readily aroused by hostility; they are almost on the lookout for a justifiable cause that will allow them a release of their own restless hostility or an identification with it. They, too, are conditioned, and many people of this group have learned to transfer their unresolved hatred of authority to another, more threatening enemy.

A common enemy has an enormous appeal because of the kindred feelings he incites. He serves to create a first uniting bond in a group. He provides for a unanimity of direction and purpose, and facilitates a basis for communication and the sharing of a goal in an often fragmented society. Even cool, intellectual individuals, unless they are emotionally of the mature, adjusted type, are swayed by an emotional appeal, especially when inflamed by a threat to national signals and symbols.

And the answer? It is unrealistic to expect men in power always to possess wisdom or full control of their ambitious drives, and therefore to be completely devoted to a preservation of peace. Political leaders seem often to walk a tightrope, trying on the one hand to keep alive the threat to national security and on the other to keep contained the fire they have stirred from bursting into an uncontrollable all-destructive blaze.

The sad course of history, with its false glamor of heroism and sacrifice, is full of evidence to prove that statesmen have been unsuccessful in securing lasting peace. But neither have religions nor philosophies nor any other school of thought been able to make peace on earth a reality. Science, avoiding the big slogans of our time and if given a chance, is most likely to succeed where the others have failed. But it must be true science. As Pavlov so well put it, "Only science, exact science about human nature itself, and the most sincere approach to it by the aid of the omnipotent scientific method, will deliver man from his present gloom, and will purge him from his contemporary shame in the sphere of inter-human relations."

My visit to the Soviet Union and my meeting with leading scientists, especially from various fields of medicine, has only strengthened my conviction that people of different cultural backgrounds and different political beliefs can work together if they share a singleness of purpose, which in the case of physicians is to understand and help people in trouble.

A young, attractive translator-guide expressed simply and succinctly the point I wish to make here. After we had doffed our coats and were entering the amphitheater of a Leningrad hospital, she turned to me and remarked, "When you (referring to our small group of visiting physicians) put on your white coats, you are not Americans, Russians, Germans . . . but only doctors."

Indeed, doctors, by their very choice of profession, indicate that they are healers, not killers; doers, not dreamers; and that they therefore do not recognize artificial barriers from their colleagues, wherever they are, in their mutual effort to fight disease and suffering. The one experience all doctors share is the knowledge of the devastating effect of illness and pain, whether of the body or the mind. The one common goal all doctors share is the need to help their patients regain a productive life and a healthy pursuit of individual happiness. Beyond this, and it is well within the realm of his chosen profession, the doctor will seek to support the work of all humans of good will that aims to achieve a peaceful, healthier, and saner society for all men.